PERSEPOLIS.

Wilber, Donald Newton
    Persepolis; the archaeology of Parsa,
seat of the Persian kings. London, Cassell
[c1969]
    xii, 120 p. illus., map, plan. 25 cm.

    Bibliography: p. 111-114.

1. Persepolis.

PERSEPOLIS

East stairway of the apadana. Carved tribute groups bring offerings from twenty-three of the lands ruled by Darius. (Iran National Tourist Organization)

PERSEPOLIS

THE ARCHAEOLOGY OF PARSA, SEAT OF THE PERSIAN KINGS

⚘ DONALD N. WILBER ⚘

CASSELL · LONDON

Pictured on endsheets: Group 23, the Ethiopian
delegation, from the east stairway of the apadana.
(Oriental Institute, University of Chicago)

CASSELL & COMPANY LTD
35 RED LION SQUARE, LONDON WC1
Melbourne, Sydney, Toronto
Johannesburg, Auckland

Copyright © 1969 by Donald Wilber
First published 1969
S.B.N. 304 93403 8

Printed in the United States of America
and bound in Great Britain
F. 169

PREFACE

Persepolis, herein called by its true name, Parsa, stands as one of the marvels of the ancient world. In the heartland of the world's first empire, it tells us much about Achaemenid times, reflecting in its architecture influences from several of the lands of that world, and showing in its carved reliefs the splendor of its kings.

Nearly forty years have passed since scientific excavations were begun at the site. With these all but completed and the attention of the Archaeological Service of Iran now turned to the task of repairing and consolidating the structures, Parsa is attracting an ever increasing number of visitors. Visitors and nonvisitors can learn a great deal about the site from the two folio volumes describing the excavations conducted from 1931 into 1939—if these volumes are available to them. No other publication deals with the site comprehensively and with adequate illustrations. The present work is intended to fill this gap. This work also contains the type of conjecture and interpretation that was deliberately avoided in the two volumes mentioned. Because of the fact that few footnotes are included here, a number of theories and conjectures are given without full acknowledgment to their makers.

Special thanks are due to Dr. Ezat O. Negahban, Director of the Institute of Archaeology, Tehran University, and of the Archaeological Museum of Iran. At my request, the manuscript was reviewed by David B. Stronach, Director of The British Institute of Persian Studies in Tehran, and by Dr. Klaus Schippmann of the University of Göttingen; I am most grateful to these scholars for their numerous and valuable suggestions. I am very grateful to Asad Behroozan of the Iran National Tourist Organization, who took many of the photographs reproduced in this book, and I also thank Malek 'Araqi, photographer of the Archaeological Service of Iran. Hassan Shahbaz, Director General, Foreign Relations' Division, Ministry of Information, also kindly assembled a group of photographs for me, and Michael Teague generously gave permission to use one of his photographs. The jacket illustration I owe to the kindness of Hans C. Seherr-Thoss; it is one of his fine color transparencies of the site.

DONALD N. WILBER

CONTENTS

ILLUSTRATIONS

MAPS AND PLANS

Aerial view of Parsa, looking northeast, in the early period of the excavations. Built on a natural-rock platform, the site covers an area of 33 acres. (Oriental Institute, University of Chicago)

The Monumental Architectural Complex
of the Achaemenid Empire — PARSA,
known to the Greeks and to Alexander
the Great as PERSEPOLIS, and
to the Persians of later centuries as the
THRONE OF JAMSHID,
which in the Persian tongue is
TAKHT-I-JAMSHID

PERSEPOLIS

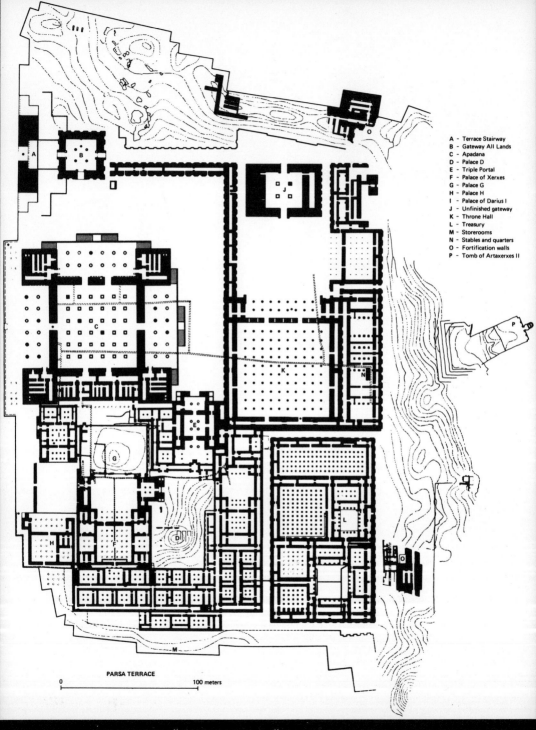

A - Terrace Stairway
B - Gateway All Lands
C - Apadana
D - Palace D
E - Triple Portal
F - Palace of Xerxes
G - Palace G
H - Palace H
I - Palace of Darius I
J - Unfinished gateway
K - Throne Hall
L - Treasury
M - Storerooms
N - Stables and quarters
O - Fortification walls
P - Tomb of Artaxerxes II

PARSA TERRACE

0   100 meters

I

PARSA: SYMBOL OF EMPIRE

Parsa and Related Sites

Driving north by car from Shiraz, an attractive, age-old city of southwestern Iran, on the modern highway that traverses the wide plain called Marv-i-Dasht, the visitor arrives abruptly at the site of Parsa—more commonly called Persepolis or Takht-i-Jamshid. Its halls and palaces rise in their orderly decay against the background of a bleak and rugged hillside that in Muslim times was named the Kuh-i-Rahmat or Mount of Mercy.

At sunset its stones glow with tints that change with the deepening dusk from yellow to pink to deep red, and once again the ancient structures appear to be engulfed by the flames of long ago. Or on another occasion, under a cloudy, wintry sky, the stones appear black, dark brown, and gray, a somber sight that evokes the lines of Omar Khayyam:

> They say the Lion and the Lizard keep
> The courts where Jamshid gloried and drank deep.

Parsa, a monumental complex of structures built to the commands of the great Achaemenid kings between 520 and about 450 B.C. to display the splendor and majesty of the world's first empire, now survives as the ruins left after its burning by Alexander the Great. Although its architectural remains, its hundreds of feet of bas-reliefs, and the inscriptions engraved on its monuments provide important clues to its history, its story is incomplete and can only be partially reconstructed from other sources.

A sense of mystery that hangs about the structures at the site can never be entirely dissipated. Although occupied for nearly two centuries, the steps, thresholds, and floors of the site show absolutely no signs of wear, and the stone utensils of the royal household show no signs of usage. Many panels

prepared for royal inscriptions were left blank—no explanation for this over-
sight exists.

Parsa is by far the most important of the four Achaemenid structures or
groups of structures in the vicinity. Sharing with the others the atmosphere of
a national, spiritual sanctuary, its halls and palace rise 40 feet above the plain
on a platform that covers 33 acres. Nine major structures occupy most of the
length—1,400 feet—and depth—nearly 1,000 feet—of the platform.

The contemporary sites include a residential area, a town, an enigmatic
structure, and a group of tombs. Below the platform of Parsa and spreading
across the plain were the residences of the ranking members of the royal court.
According to Greek sources, this very spacious area was surrounded by a
double wall and separated from the platform by a wide moat.

From the foot of the platform, the ancient highway led north and then to the
east around the end spur of the Mount of Mercy. At this point, on the bank
of the Pulvar River and some three miles from Parsa, was the second site, the
town of Stakhra. Today only scanty remains of post-Achaemenid construction
dot this area. The river may be crossed here at a ford. Farther along, some six
miles from Parsa, a rock cliff 500 feet long and as much as 200 feet in height
is reached. This cliff, the third site, is called the Naqsh-i-Rustam, or Picture of
Rustam, from the modern opinion that a bas-relief of the Sassanian period
depicts Rustam, a legendary hunter. Actually, there are three such reliefs, two
with the figures on horseback: the investiture of Ardashir I (third century A.D.),

The Parsa platform, as viewed looking west from the hillside above. The protective shelter

the triumph of Shapur I (second half, third century), and Varahran III with his family, who are not mounted.

Carved into the face of this cliff are the rock-cut tombs of four of the Achaemenid rulers associated with Parsa, and, below them, the bas-reliefs of later historical periods. In front of the cliff arises a structure of the Achaemenid period, the so-called Ka'ba-i-Zardusht, or Shrine of Zarathushtra. The cliff of Naqsh-i-Rustam is not visible from Parsa, as the direct line of sight is intercepted by the northern slopes of the Mount of Mercy.

Parsa is primarily the reflection of the commands of two Achaemenid kings: Darius I, and his son and successor, Xerxes. Darius took great pride in his family tree. He was proud of being a Persian (Parsa), of being of Persian descent, and of being an Aryan of Aryan lineage. His lineage went much farther back than that of Alexander, who eventually destroyed his effort to attain immortality through architecture. Darius' ancestors had arrived in this region of the ancient world nearly one thousand years before Parsa was built.

The Aryans

The upland Iranian plateau, a vast region that today comprises the countries of Iran and Afghanistan, has an average altitude of over 4,000 feet above sea level. Marked more by barren ranges and arid deserts than by fertile areas, and with widely spaced towns located along its infrequent perennial streams,

over the east stair of the apadana is no longer in place. (Persian Gulf Command)

the plateau has always been a place of passage between remote Asia and the lands around the Mediterranean Sea. From the most ancient times, peoples from the heart of Asia have moved south and west to the plateau and beyond. Only the caravans of the traders came in peace. Nomadic warriors, astride horses, whose daily progress was geared to the slow pace of their flocks and herds, came in search of grazing grounds. Powerful armies passed by, leaving ruined cities and slaughtered inhabitants in their wakes.

Some centuries before the opening of the first millennium B.C. Aryan tribes crossed the Oxus River, which bounded the northeastern limits of the plateau. Some of them turned toward the Indian subcontinent, where they overcame the local, darker skinned people and established an enduring social distinction, that of caste, a term that came from the word *varna*, or color. Other tribes moved westward across the plateau, probably in successive waves with long intervals of time between each such movement.

It is certain that these people were Aryans. They so name themselves in their religious works, fragmentarily preserved, and the rulers of the Achaemenid dynasty called themselves Aryans. Among the Aryan tribes that came to the plateau was a group who gave it their name—the Iranians. Iran and Arya(n) are the same linguistically, although Iran as the country name did not appear until after the Achaemenid period.

Long and sustained effort has been devoted in trying to reconstruct the religion and the social structure of the Aryans prior to their arrival on the plateau. The chief source has been the *Avesta,* a compendium of very ancient hymns and other documents. Their local divinities were the sun, the sky, and

Quarry adjacent to the northern edge of the platform. Voids indicate where large monoliths have been removed. Vertical and diagonal channels attest to the use of wedges. (Donald N. Wilber)

An unfinished column drum. The building pieces were composed of hard limestone rock, containing bitumen and ranging in color from gray to brown to black. (Donald N. Wilber)

other objects and aspects of nature. The people were nomadic cattle breeders who practiced limited agriculture, and rode horseback.

The evidence for the arrival of the Aryans on the plateau, and even of their movement as far as the plains of Mesopotamia, derives from inscriptions in non-Indo-European languages. One, about 1370 B.C., contains the names of Aryan gods, while others include Aryan words. These earliest arrivals were largely absorbed by the indigenous populations, and it was only after the appearance of the Iranians, whose tribes included the Mada, or Amadai (Medes), and the Parsa (Persians), that the Aryans were sufficiently numerous to be able to impose their will on local areas. Since the powerful armies of the state of Assyria already had campaigned throughout the regions on the western slopes of the plateau, defeating these indigenous peoples and deporting large numbers of them, the task of the newcomers was relatively easy. Eventually, however, they, in their turn, came up against Assyrian might.

The Parsa are first recorded, in the form Parsua, in an Assyrian cuneiform

5

Carefully sized rocks were fitted against the native rock with jigsaw puzzle precision. The columns of the apadana loom above the terrace wall. (Iran National Tourist Organization)

Two-headed animal, resembling a lion, was probably an experimental form that never found its place atop a column. Ears and horns were affixed to the sockets in the heads. (Persian Gulf Command)

Another experimental capital, possibly a griffin, a fabulous creature that is half eagle and half lion. Two small holes were once carefully cleaned out and filled with patches of stone. (Iran Ministry of Information)

Detail from column capital showing head of bull. Ear, now missing, was made of separate piece of stone. (Iran National Tourist Organization)

inscription of 843 that relates to a campaign of Shalmaneser III and places them some distance to the southwest of present Lake Rizayeh (also Lake Urmia). Possibly there were two other groups of Parsa, one far to the south and the other a long distance to the west of the group named in the inscription. Following this interpretation, the Parsa of special interest were those who were in contact with the Elamites, an indigenous people whose habitat was the southwestern corner of the plateau and, in particular, the city of Susa. Indeed, in 690 the Parsa allied themselves with the Elamites to fight against Assyria.

The Medes are mentioned in an Assyrian inscription of 835. This tribe, or group of subtribes, fought with each other as well as with the forces of Urartu and the kingdom of Assyria. One of the leaders of the Medes, Dayaukku, attempted to unite them, but the time was not propitious. Then, in 673, Khshathrita, known to the Greek historians as Phraortes, succeeded in bringing the Medes together against Assyria and in imposing Median sovereignty on Parsa.

7

Life-size statue of a watchdog, now in the Museum of Archaeology in Tehran. (Archaeological Service of Iran)

His son Uvakhshtra (Cyaxares), however, took Parsa into an alliance against what should have been the common enemy, Assyria.

In 614 Cyaxares moved against Assyria and took the city of Ashur, and in 612 he razed great Nineveh to the ground. There was a pause while this great booty was distributed, and then Cyaxares moved as far west as Lydia. In 585 he returned to absorb the kingdom of Urartu at Lake Van and to establish the frontier of his realm along the Araxes River. Thus it was that the Medes broke out of the mold of a petty principality in the mountains that flanked the western edge of the plateau to become a power strong enough to destroy the mighty kingdom of Assyria.

Kurush (Cyrus II), a Persian, a descendant of Hakhamanish (Achaemenes), appears in 559 as the king of Anshan. Anshan was the aboriginal name of a region that was to include Parsa and Huja (Elam). Cyrus was a vassal of the Medes. In 555 he allied himself with the Babylonian king and in about 549 he defeated the advancing forces of the Median king, Astyages, in battle. By 546 he had taken over Elam, which had failed to recover from the devastation visited on it by the Assyrians much earlier. Acquiring other allies, Cyrus marched against Croesus of Lydia and captured the renowned city of Sardis.

Stone tablets bearing cuneiform inscriptions of Xerxes in Old Persian, Elamite, and Akkadian. Trilingual records such as these attest to kingship and
religious piety, but leave few clues to history. (Archaeological Service of Iran)

On his way back to his homeland he turned aside to take Babylon in the year
539.

Cyrus took as his capital Hagmatana—the modern town of Hamadan, which
was known to the Greeks as Ecbatana—the former Median capital. But by this
time construction was probably well advanced at his own site, possibly called
Paishiyauvada (Pasargadae). This site was a well-watered mountain valley in
Parsa, and according to the Greek historians was at or near the place where
he had defeated Astyages. Its structures, scattered about the site, included his
own tomb, which housed his body after his death in battle in 530.

Cyrus is usually regarded as the outstanding figure of the fifteen rulers,
some rather ephemeral, of the Achaemenid dynasty. By claiming to be the
successor of Astyages and welcoming the Medes to share in his state, he established close and enduring Persian-Median relations. The people of the many
conquered lands were generously treated, and their customs and religious
beliefs were respected. Cyrus worshipped at their altars and on occasion rein-

9

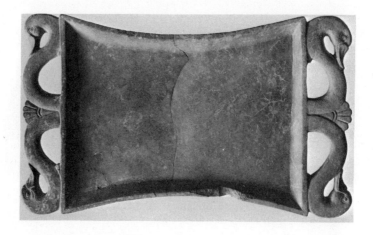

A gray stone tray with handles in the form of swans' heads. Since the site was seldom occupied, many artifacts at Parsa show little wear. (Oriental Institute, University of Chicago)

stated their own lords in office. The Book of Ezra records his benevolence toward the Jews.

Cyrus was succeeded by his son Kambujiya (Cambyses II), whose fairly brief reign ran to 522 and was marked by his successful invasion of Egypt. Then Darayavaush (Darius), a member of another branch of the Achaemenid clan, came to power by defeating Gaumata, a false claimant to the throne, with the help of a number of the noble families. This triumph was recorded in carved inscriptions in three languages: Old Persian, Elamite, and Akkadian (Babylonian). That in his own language, Old Persian, was 414 lines. This record was on the face of a cliff rising abruptly above an age-old caravan road about sixty-five miles from Ecbatana at a place called Behistun (Old Persian, Baga-Stana, place of the God). Some 225 feet above the roadway are to be seen the figures in relief of Darius and his captives, the false king and a number of rebels. The inscriptions themselves cover an area 59 feet wide and 25 feet high; they give the details of his victories over all the rebels and supply information about his ethical views.

The inscriptions were first reached and copied by Henry C. Rawlinson, then a British lieutenant, between 1836 and 1847. The decipherment of Old Persian was actually undertaken before the end of the eighteenth century, but little progress was made until after the middle of the nineteenth century. Conso-

The east side of the gateway All Lands is guarded by two massive winged bulls with human heads. The forequarters project forward from the piles of masonry. Inscriptions above the wings state, "I (am) Xerxes, the great King, King of Kings." (Iran Ministry of Information)

nants and vowels were identified by making comparisons of the cuneiform signs on inscriptions of Darius and Xerxes, noting the relative positions of phrases assumed, correctly, to mean "great king, king of kings."

The Builders and Their Descendants

The brief outline of the activities of the Achaemenid rulers that follows is drawn from Greek sources, notably the *Histories* of Herodotus. It should be remembered that the size of the Persian armies is greatly exaggerated by the Greek writers.

After Darius had solidified his hold on the throne and had ordered construction undertaken at Parsa, he took command of his forces and headed west. In 512 he crossed the Bosporus and subdued Thrace. He then moved across the Danube, but withdrew to his homeland without consolidating his conquests.

Entrance stairway and gateway, or portico, All Lands. The structure originally had a roof supported by four columns. (Persian Gulf Command)

Columns and masonry, the gateway All Lands. The masonry wall at left shows that the stones were only roughly dressed where they fitted against walls of mud brick. (Iran National Tourist Organization)

Nineteenth-century engraving of a column base, a section, and a capital from gateway All Lands. (*Voyage en Perse de MM. Eugene Flandin, Peintre, et Pascal Coste, Architecte*)

Detail of a column capital from gateway All Lands, now in the Archaeological Museum at Tehran. (Archaeological Service of Iran)

Finding that the Greek colonies in Asia Minor had been aided by mainland states in attempted uprisings against the Achaemenid garrisons, he launched two more campaigns against the mainland—in 492 and 490. This last venture ended in disaster at the battle of Marathon, which was followed by a Persian withdrawal.

Xerxes I succeeded his father, Darius, in 486. With a force that Herodotus claimed numbered 1,700,000 men and supported by a great fleet, he led a campaign against Greece which was marked by the capture of Athens and the burning of its Acropolis in 480. However, after Xerxes' fleet was destroyed in the battle of Salamis and his ground forces beaten in the battle of Plataea, he withdrew to Asia Minor. Warfare between the Greek city states and the Achaemenid empire did not end, but gradually relations became less ardently hostile.

Artaxerxes I followed his father in 465 and reigned until 424. The decay of the empire was reflected in revolts in Egypt and other satrapies, and it was not until the period of Artaxerxes III, who ruled from 359 until 338, that the earlier limits of the empire were briefly restored.

Ineffectual Darius III came to the throne just as Alexander, the son of Philip of Macedonia, was extending his control over the Greek mainland. Shortly thereafter Alexander landed in Asia. At Issus, just inland from the Syrian coast, Alexander led his forces to rout an enormous Achaemenid army commanded by Darius III. When the tide of battle ran against him, Darius fled the field, abandoning his wife, mother, and an infant son to the victor.

Alexander then led his troops down the Mediterranean coast to acquire Egypt and to be received as a god. Returning, and retracing his route through Syria, he headed east, crossing the Euphrates and Tigris rivers. East of the Tigris, at Gaugamela, he met and defeated another Persian army, said to have numbered 1,040,000 men as compared with his own 47,000 soldiers. A detailed record of this battle survives; it names all the major contingents of the Persian armies. Once again, Darius fled.

Following his victory at Gaugamela, Alexander marched south to receive the capitulation of Babylon, and then went due east to Susa, which had already opened its gates to his advance guard. The treasures in its palaces amounted to 40,000 talents of silver—estimated at $1,200 for each talent—and 9,000 talents of gold. Continuing through the mountains to the east of Susa, Alexander's passage was opposed by fierce tribesmen. But his forces brushed aside these opponents and entered the land of Parsa, racing against time to seize Parsa itself before it could be sacked by its own garrison. It was reached on February 1, 330, and was surrendered to Alexander. The settlement below the platform of Parsa was ruthlessly looted and its inhabitants massacred. Alexander's historians recorded the enormous booty: 120,000 silver talents, 8,000 talents of gold, and an inexhaustible supply of jewels and objects of gold.

After making a brief trip some forty-five miles to the north to take over the treasures of Cyrus at Pasargadae, Alexander returned to Parsa, which was soon engulfed in flames. Some sources record that the fiery destruction was by design, others state it was accidental. Flavius Arrianus (Arrian), who obtained his material from a lost account by Aristobulus, a historian in Alexander's train, had a very firm opinion. Alexander had the palace Persica set on fire to punish the Persians for what they had done in their invasions of Greece: the devastation of Athens, the burning of temples, and the slaughter of the Greeks.

Next Alexander ventured north and then east in pursuit of Darius III. He found only his remains: the ruler had been killed by his own attendants. Darius' body was sent back to Parsa for burial in the royal tombs. Alexander then turned his face toward the rising sun, embarking on the incredible journey that would take him to unknown India. There, his aim of marching to the world's end was frustrated by the unwillingness of his soldiers to venture farther into the unknown. After the march back to Susa, which took many months and was marked by great hardships, there apparently was some time for relaxation and leisure pursuits. Alexander paid a return visit to the tomb of Cyrus, only to find that it had been broken open and rifled since his first visit. Arrianus reports this visit in great detail, stating that Alexander had the damage repaired, and the door of the tomb blocked up and covered with clay. Into this clay coating he set his royal seal as a guarantee that the tomb would remain inviolate. This same historian, writing long after the events, gives a description of the tomb, stating that it was in an irrigated park, surrounded by groves of trees and meadows of deep grass. The tomb itself, a rectangular edifice with a stone roof, was raised on a base of stones—details that are in full accord with the surviving structure.

Although the holocaust of Parsa brought the Achaemenid empire to a sudden and decisive end, there was yet some value in its destruction for very distant, future generations. The masonry elements of its structures and its bas-reliefs were actually protected by the burned debris and the wind-blown dust of the following centuries. They were certainly better protected than they would have been if there had been any unburned buildings remaining above ground, offering inviting opportunities for later builders to carry away the stones.

The columns and north stairway of the apadana, viewed from the gateway All Lands. The original hall, which held ten thousand people, was supported by thirty-six columns. A monolithic ablution basin is in the foreground. (Persian Gulf Command)

II

THE ACHAEMENIDS
AND THEIR RELATIONSHIP
TO PARSA

Inscriptions

Parsa is assumed to have been the spiritual sanctuary of the vast Achaemenid empire. In part this assumption is based on the bas-reliefs that depict the rulers enthroned below the symbol, or figure, of the god Ahuramazda—the God of the Aryans. It certainly was the sacred site where the kings were crowned and buried and where tribute from all the lands of the empire was presented on the occasion of the New Year's festival. New Year's Day was that of the vernal equinox, either March 21 or 22. Its reliefs depict the king borne on a portable throne, and a study of the very specialized subject of cosmic kingship suggests that the movement of this throne was a part of the ritual which marked the New Year's festival. It has been suggested, without convincing evidence, that the orientation of the platform and of its structures and the different levels of the platform were related to a function of the site as one for observing and recording the movement of the heavens, especially the occurrences of the equinoxes and the solstices.

The inscriptions at Parsa provide few details about the purpose and functions of the buildings on the site. It is very unlikely that the recorded rock-cut inscriptions on cliff faces will be augmented by new finds; the chances of discovering additional clay tablets at Achaemenid sites are better.

It is somewhat surprising that no Achaemenid writings comparable with those of contemporary Greece have survived. Possibly, such lengthy docu-

Column base and lower shaft from the apadana. Thirteen columns
remain, each 67 feet high. (Iran National Tourist Organization)

ments never existed. The inscriptions carved for these rulers on cliff faces, on
tombs, and on, or related to, architectural monuments total about 5,800 words.
With the notable exceptions of the long rock-cut inscription of Darius at
Behistun and the inscription on his tomb, these are largely repetitious statements of kingship and relationship, of religious piety, and of lists of lands
under Achaemenid dominion. This material is of very limited value to the historian. The name Parsa, for example, has been found only at the platform itself.

Of the total wordage of these inscriptions, there are fewer than five hundred
words, and many of these are personal names, place names, and the names of
months. Pity the linguists who have tried to reconstruct the grammar of Old
Persian from this sparse material, and praise them for their success!

The carved inscriptions of these rulers were usually trilingual, executed in
cuneiform signs in Old Persian, Elamite, and Akkadian (Babylonian). What
scholars call Old Persian was the vernacular speech of the Achaemenid rulers.
The language belonged to the Iranian branch of the Indo-Iranian, or Aryan,
group, one of the main divisions of the Indo-European family of languages. At
Parsa and elsewhere Old Persian was employed only for royal inscriptions,
with Elamite and Aramaic as the written languages used at the court.

The north stairway of the apadana, showing long lines of Persian, Median, and Susian guards. The faces have been badly mutilated by successive generations of Muslims. (Persian Gulf Command)

Tribute delegations depicted in bas-reliefs on the east stairway. Figures such as these on both the north and east stairways bring gifts from twenty-three of the lands ruled by Darius. (Persian Gulf Command)

Everything we may hope to learn about Parsa must come from the site itself: from the information contained in inscriptions on the structures, inscriptions on stones and objects, such as plates of gold and silver, found in the excavations, and from thousands of unbaked clay tablets that were unearthed in two areas of the site.

Some thirty thousand tablets and fragments of tablets were uncovered in 1933 and 1934 in the northern fortification wall area. Dating between 510 and 494, complete tablets are only 1½ by 1¼ inches in size, and the proportion of whole tablets to fragments is very low. In 1938 and 1939 the excavators found some 750 larger tablets and fragments of tablets, dating from 492 to 460, in the ruins of the Treasury. The dates of some of the tablets were established because they included the year of a ruler's reign. Of the Treasury tablets, only 114 contained enough textual material to warrant translation. In a remarkably painstaking and comprehensive publication by George C. Cameron, *Persepolis Treasury Tablets*, translations were given and conclusions drawn from this material.

A section of the north stairway, with tribute delegations. (Persian Gulf Command)

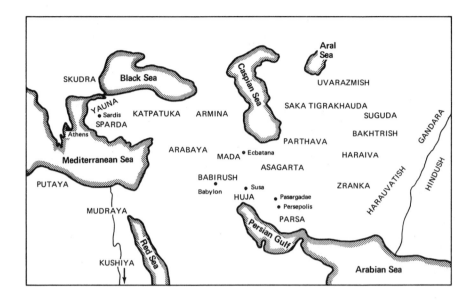

Parsa and the twenty-three lands held by Darius early in his reign. The representatives of these lands are shown on the reliefs of the apadana stairways.

Although all the tablets from the fortification wall area have not been studied, thus far no material of historical significance has appeared. According to Cameron, the material includes "no treaties, chronicles, annals, letters to or from satraps, or edicts to distant outposts of the realm."

The Treasury tablets were the records, in Elamite, of the treasurers of Parsa, whose domain covered the site of Parsa and the region of the same name. Most of the tablets fall into one of two categories: letters requesting payment for work completed and memoranda calling for reimbursement for payments made. The translator of the tablets has outlined the steps taken in the preparation. Officials gave oral instructions to scribes who wrote them down in Aramaic on papyrus or parchment. At intervals these Aramaic notes were sent to the Treasury and transferred to a more permanent medium by scribes, who translated the notes into Elamite and then cut the records in cuneiform signs on clay tablets. It is assumed that these scribes were Elamites who had been moved to Parsa from Susa, another royal seat. Official seals attested to the authenticity of the records engraved on the tablets. People who received payment included employees of the Treasury, attendants and servants at Parsa, and workers engaged in erecting and decorating the structures.

21

These tablets make two general contributions to our knowledge of the site: the dates when two rulers, Darius and Xerxes, were active there and information about workers at the site.

Since the Achaemenids failed to write their own history, we remain very largely dependent on accounts by Greek writers, some contemporary with the Achaemenid rulers and others of much later dates. These writers had little reason to be sympathetic or impartial toward an empire that had engulfed the Greek colonies of Asia and had repeatedly attacked the mainland of Greece. In addition, much of their information was of doubtful reliability, based on traditions, myths that grew up around distant incidents, and "facts" that had been handed down over many generations.

Greek writers, such as Arrianus, employed the term "barbarian" as interchangeable with "Persian," but in those years barbarian meant only foreigner or alien. It has been only in modern times that the concept of the Persians as barbarians, that is uncivilized as compared with the Greeks, has gained some currency. Actually, the Persians seem to have looked down on the commercially minded Greeks, and it is clear that in such aspects of public life as

The east stairway of the apadana. Chariots, horses, and attendants precede the dignitaries of the realm. Concealed by earth until its excavation in 1932, the figures on the east stairway are much better preserved than those on the north stairway. (Oriental Institute, University of Chicago)

The central panel of the east stairway of the apadana, depicting Persian and Median guards. The Medes wear belted knee-length coats and trousers fitted tightly at the ankles. The Persians wear long flowing robes and fluted hats. The symbol of the god Ahuramazda appears above them. (Iran National Tourist Organization)

administration, stable government, and tolerance of different races and creeds the Persian achievements outshone those of the Greek city states.

The Greeks knew of Parsa only through rumor, although they were well informed about the towns of Babylon, Ecbatana, and Susa. Aeschylus, a contemporary of Xerxes I, called the site Perseptolis, "destroyer of cities," a reference to the burning of Athens by Xerxes. His term became corrupted to Persepolis, alleged to mean "town of the Persians," although the correct form would be Persopolis.

Ctesias, the Greek physician of Artaxerxes II, who lived at the royal court for twenty years, never saw the site and did not mention it in his writings. A contemporary of his, Xenophon, referred to it as Persai. In much later times

Parsa became Pars or Fars, with the letters P and F interchangeable in the Arabic alphabet then in use. From these versions the larger world called the country Persia, unaware that its true name was Iran.

Long reliance on Greek sources has led to a total neglect of certain material from Achaemenid sources. The names of the rulers and officials and place names have become familiar in Greek versions, even in faulty translations of these names. Here we may hope to correct the record. The names here listed were throne names; the personal names of the rulers are not known. It should be noted that those who assumed the throne name of a predecessor did not add distinguishing numerals, as we do, but identified themselves by citing their genealogy in their inscriptions.

Parsa is so named in inscriptions on the entrance portico. Work was first undertaken by Darayavaush, "Holding firm the good" (Darius I), who ruled from 522 until 486, and who proudly identified himself as the "son of Vishtaspa [Hystaspes], Hakhamanishiya [an Achaemenid], Parsa [a Persian], Parshaya [son of a Persian], Ariya [an Aryan], cisa Ariya [of Aryan lineage]." His work was carried on by his son Khshayarsha, "Hero among kings" (Xerxes I, 486–465), and a grandson, Artakhshasa, "Having a kingdom of justice" (Artaxerxes I, 465–425).

The inscriptions executed for the Achaemenid rulers provide the names of the lands of the empire and some basic facts about the people and their country. Two predecessors of Darius, Ariyaramna and Arshama, recorded that Parsa possessed good horses and good people.

Darius gives a much fuller account of himself than do any of the other rulers. A portion of his inscription at Behistun reads:

> I was not a Lie-follower, I was not a doer of wrong . . . . According to righteousness I conducted myself. Neither to the weak or to the powerful did I do wrong. The man who cooperated with my house, him I rewarded well; whoso did injury, him I punished well.

The inscriptions on his tomb at Naqsh-i-Rustam echo similar sentiments and then develop his personality and attributes:[1]

> I am not hot-tempered. What things develop in my anger, I hold firmly

[1]These inscriptions are translated by Roland G. Kent in *Old Persian: Grammar, Texts, Lexicon.*

Detail from the central panel, east stair. The scene of the lion attacking the bull was symbolically related to the spring equinox. (Iran National Tourist Organization)

A close-up of the head of the lion reveals the finely chiseled detail of the east stairway figures. (Iran National Tourist Organization)

As on the north stairway, the groups on the east stairway bring tribute from twenty-three of the lands ruled by Darius. The delegations range from three to six members. The leader of each group is escorted by a Persian or Mede, who clasps his hand. A cypress tree divides each group from the next.

Groups 4, 5, and 6, showing (top to bottom) Aryan, Babylonian, and Lydian delegations. Parts of groups 2 and 3 are shown at the right. (Iran National Tourist Organization)

Group 11, Pointed-hat Scythians; Group 12, Ionians, possibly carrying beehives and skeins of colored wool. Parts of group 10, Egyptians, are shown at the top. (Iran National Tourist Organization)

Groups 13, 14, and 15, representing the Parthian, Gandarian, and Bactrian delegations. (Iran National Tourist Organization)

Groups 16, 17, and 18, the Sagartians, Chorasmians, and Indians. (Iran National Tourist Organization)

Group 23, the Ethiopian delegation, exhibiting distinctively negroid hair and features. The figure on the left carries an elephant's tusk and leads an okapi. (Oriental Institute, University of Chicago)

under control by my thinking power . . . What a man says against a man, that does not convince me, until he satisfies the Ordinance of Good Regulations. What a man does or performs (for me) according to his (natural) powers, (therewith) I am satisfied and my pleasure is abundant, and I am well satisfied. Of such a sort is my understanding and my command: when what has been done by me thou shalt see or hear of, both in the palace and in the war-camp, this is my activity over and above my thinking power and my understanding.

This indeed is my activity: inasmuch as my body has the strength, as battle fighter I am a good battle fighter . . . Trained am I both with hands and with feet. As a horseman I am a good horseman. As a bowman I am a good bowman both afoot and on horseback. As a spearman I am a good spearman both afoot and on horseback . . . O menial, vigorously make thou known of what sort I am, and of what sort my skillfulnesses, and of what sort my superiority. Let not that seem false to thee which has been heard by thy ears.

Darius probably dictated the substance of the inscription in his native tongue (Old Persian) to a scribe, with the certain knowledge that his words would be carved in Old Persian, Elamite and Akkadian.

Culture

Royal inscriptions provide only fragmentary information about the Achaemenids. The most comprehensive source again is the accounts by Herodotus of the campaigns of Darius and Xerxes against mainland Greece. The author left his home in Asia Minor about 457 and traveled for at least ten years collecting background material. It is certain that he knew Asia Minor well and that he spent a considerable length of time in Egypt and Libya. He probably visited Mesopotamia, too, but it is unlikely that he reached the Iranian plateau. He certainly did talk with Persians to obtain what he himself calls firsthand knowledge of them.

Echoing the carved words of Darius, Herodotus wrote that Persian youths were instructed in three things alone: to ride, to draw the bow, and to speak the truth. He wrote of the Persian prowess in arms, of their inclination to luxury, and of their eagerness to adopt foreign customs—"they have learnt unnatural lust from the Greeks." Concerning religion, he wrote that they have

Detail of group 15, a Bactrian delegate leading a camel. (Iran National Tourist Organization)

Detail of group 18, an Indian tribute bearer with baskets and vases. (Iran National Tourist Organization)

no images of the gods, no temples and no altars, and offer sacrifices to the sun, moon, earth, fire, and water.

Herodotus wrote of the royal road that ran between Susa and Sardis, a distance of 1,500 miles. Official messages were carried by riders, who drew fresh horses from post stations. The historian gave his versions of the meanings of the names of the Achaemenid rulers. Thus, Darius was rendered as "Worker," Xerxes as "Warrior," and Artaxerxes as "Great Warrior." From these mistranslations it appears that Herodotus drew on some unreliable sources, although his accounts of the manner by which Darius put down revolts and gained the throne strongly suggest that he had seen a copy of the Behistun inscription translated into a language that he could read.

Herodotus wrote that Darius divided his empire into twenty administrative units called satrapies. The word satrap does not occur in Achaemenid inscriptions, which employ the word "land" to define subject and tributary areas. The governors of the "lands" came from noble Persian families. From sources other than Herodotus it appears that these posts tended to become hereditary. In fact, this system of a monarchy supported by a number of semi-independent provincial lords continued throughout many centuries in Iran and was broken up only in the twentieth century.

Again according to Herodotus, the army was composed of six corps, each of sixty thousand men in six divisions; there was also the personal bodyguard of the rulers, the "Immortals," who were so called because their number was always maintained at ten thousand.

Agriculture flourished and justice was fairly administered. The legal code of Darius, based on the Code of Hammurabi, has not been preserved, although it is reflected in the autobiographical inscriptions of Darius. It was respectfully mentioned throughout the ancient world, with the Book of Daniel writing of "the law of the Medes and Persians which altereth not." Ethnic groups within the bounds of the empire were permitted to practice their religions and were aided in the building of new temples, such as one at Jerusalem.

Herodotus gives figures of the amount of tribute, or taxes, paid in gold or silver by the satraps. Tax farmers probably collected payments in precious metals or in kind, with the monetary unit, the *daric*, so named after Darius by the Greeks.

At the royal court and among the noble families the chivalrous spirit so well expressed by Darius was preserved, but here was a strong impact from the so-called "oriental" modes of life and ways of thought common to highly cultured Mesopotamia. In those ancient times, peoples distant in space and in heritage had firmly held views about each other.

31

The Assyrians, the mighty predecessors of the Achaemenids, were, as their inscriptions and pictorial reliefs reveal, cruel, boastful, and self-centered. Quite in contrast, the Achaemenids appear to have felt their universal mission was to bring order to the ends of the world. This world was held in trust by these rulers; many petty kings were permitted to exercise their previous authority, and trade and commerce flourished under a blanket of security.

One of the most puzzling aspects of Achaemenid power is that these experienced warriors were, after their earlier conquests, less than inspired in military strategy and tactics. Xerxes seems to have believed that he could overwhelm the Greek mainland by sheer numbers of soldiers and ships. When progress was held up by a small force of Greeks, his generals were not content to leave a body of troops to besiege the place while the main army moved ahead, but insisted on its reduction.

After the first defeat of Darius III by Alexander, the Persian ruler selected the broad plain at Gaugamela as a battleground, and even had parts of it leveled to make the terrain suitable for his cavalry. The standard battle array of Alexander was to place cavalry on both flanks of the infantry phalanx. During battle the right wing pivoted toward the phalanx, thus taking the center of the enemy from the flank. Had his forces been as enormous as stated by the Greek writers, Darius III should have been able to arrange reserve forces of infantry and cavalry in great depth, and as the battle wore on, call on these reserves to overwhelm the Greeks by sheer force of numbers.

Religion

The identification of Parsa as the spiritual heart of the empire is related to the religious beliefs of the Achaemenid rulers. Scholars have drawn on every kind of evidence, some building elaborate frameworks on scanty foundations, but there has been no general agreement among them on this subject.

Keeping in mind the character of the early Aryan divinities, any investigation of the old Persian religion should begin by seeing what the rulers themselves had to say about their gods, as recorded in their inscriptions. Ariyaramna mentions "the great god, Ahuramazda," and Arshama speaks of the "great god, greatest of gods, Ahuramazda." Darius employs this same formula, and adds another "Ahuramazda, together with the gods of the royal house."

Xerxes calls on "Ahuramazda, together with the gods" and worships "Ahuramazda and Arta reverently." Artaxerxes I and Darius II call on Ahuramazda for blessing, while Artaxerxes II appeals to "Ahuramazda, Anaitis

Northwest view of the Throne Hall. The structure is named for its reliefs of the ruler enthroned. (Iran Ministry of Information)

View of the Throne Hall, showing rows of column bases. The roof was supported by ten rows of ten columns each. (Iran Ministry of Information)

(Anahita), and Mithras (Mithra)," and Artaxerxes III calls on "Ahuramazda and the god Mithras."

Anahita and Mithra were Aryan divinities, who won great popularity among non-Aryans and whose cults survived throughout much of the ancient world for centuries after the end of the Achaemenid empire. This was not, however, the future of Ahuramazda, who is named by Darius on his rock-cut inscription at Behistun as the "god of the Aryans." Arta, always associated with Ahuramazda, was a god of justice.

The material available from a variety of sources indicates that the early Achaemenids—Darius for example—worshiped fire at altars, offered animal sacrifices, prepared and drank *haoma* (a stimulant), believed in a pervading dualism of the world in which conflict they held fast to the truth and scorned the lie, and had certain sanctuaries. It is of interest to contrast this information with what Herodotus wrote:

> They have no images of gods, no temples or altars, and consider the use of them a sign of folly. This comes, I think, from their not believing the gods to have the same nature with man, as the Greeks imagine. Their wont, however, is to ascend the summits of the loftiest mountains, and there to offer sacrifice to Jupiter, which is the name they give to the whole circuit of the firmament. They likewise offer to the sun and moon, to the earth, to fire, to water, and to the winds. These are the only gods whose worship has come down to them from ancient times . . .
>
> To these gods the Persians offer sacrifice in the following manner: they raise no altar, light no fire, pour no libations.

Herodotus then presented the manner of sacrifices in some detail, stating that there must always be a Magus present. "The Magi are a very peculiar race . . . [they] kill animals of all kinds with their own hands, excepting dogs and men." He also wrote, although not in connection with religion, "The most disgraceful thing in the world they [the Persians] think, is to tell a lie."

Herodotus' words reflect some understanding of aspects of the Zoroastrian religion, although he had heard neither of its prophet and founder Zarathushtra nor of Ahuramazda, its greatest god.

The prophet Zarathushtra, known later to the Greeks as Zoroaster, is believed to have been active in eastern Iran shortly after 600 B.C. As a priest of the old Aryan faith, he found little honor in his homeland, and after migrating, he began a successful mission with the conversion of Vishtaspa, a local ruler.

Surviving elements of a massive guardian bull, which stood at the north end of the Throne Hall. (Persian Gulf Command)

Our knowledge of the person and of the teachings of Spitama ("White," his clan name) Zarathushtra comes from the *Avesta*, a fragmentary collection of hymns, legal codes, and rituals of various dates. It was not written down for many centuries; in fact, the oldest surviving manuscript dates from the thirteenth century A.D.

Zarathushtra, claiming to be the chosen one of Ahuramazda, taught the dualism of Good and Evil, with man free to choose between them, and he advocated Good Thoughts, Good Words, and Good Deeds.

One may read that the prophet instructed his followers to abstain from worshiping the cults of the *daivas*, or demons, from sacrificing beef, and from the use of haoma.

The Aryans, whose way of life was reflected in the *Avesta*, were sedentary cattle breeders and farmers. They held cattle in very high respect and showed only somewhat less respect for dogs, horses, and camels—the prophet's own name means "to care for camels." They worshiped fire and water and considered the pollution of the earth a great evil. It is probable that the daivas

35

were the ancient Aryan nature divinities. In a culture that held cattle in such respect and awe, it would have been wrong to offer them as sacrifices.

Zoroastrianism, sometimes called Mazdaism, stood for lofty ethical values. It differed from the several monotheistic religions that arose in the ancient East by associating lesser gods with the greatest of gods. In later times, notably in the Sassanian period, it became the state religion; it continued to be a vital faith until some centuries after the invasion of Iran by the Arab armies and the conversion of most of the people to Islam. Dedicated groups of believers moved to India, where they became known as Parsees, while smaller groups in the more remote parts of Iran continued to practice their faith in secret. Nowadays, however, Zoroastrianism is well accepted in Iran, with strong communities of believers at Tehran, Yazd, and Kerman.

Much has been written about Zoroastrianism in Achaemenid times, but many questions remain unanswered, perhaps unanswerable. For example, was Darius a Zoroastrian? The strongest affirmative evidence exists in the similarity of statements in his inscriptions, in which truth is praised and the lie condemned, and the teachings of Zarathushtra. Although none of the inscriptions of the Achaemenid kings mention Zarathushtra, they all exalt Ahuramazda above all the other gods. It seems reasonable to suppose that in the reign of Darius there was as yet no organized church with an immutable dogma, and that the teachings of Zarathushtra comprised a more recent layer superimposed on the traditional Aryan religious practices.

The sacrificing of animals continued under the Achaemenid rulers: Herodotus describes large scale sacrifices ordered by Xerxes. And it was, as Herodotus wrote, the Magi who were in charge of these sacrifices. The Magi were one of the several Iranian tribes who had moved onto the plateau and were distinguished from the others by having acquired exclusive rights to exercising priestly functions.

Prior to the time of the Achaemenids and during their empire, the Aryans and the Iranians worshiped fire. On the carved reliefs on the tombs of these rulers fire altars are shown with the figure of Ahuramazda hovering over the altar. Seal stones of the period also show fire altars, and there are rock-hewn altars of similar appearance, although probably much later in date, adjacent to Persepolis.

The Old Persian word for sanctuary, *ayadana*, is found in the inscription of Darius at Behistun. Two very similar tower-like structures—one, poorly preserved, at Pasargadae, and the other, the so-called Ka'ba-i-Zardusht at Naqsh-i-Rustam—are believed to have been ayadanas. In plan form and in section

Relief of ruler Artaxerxes I enthroned beneath a canopy on door jamb of the Throne Hall. (Iran Ministry of Information)

The legs of the ruler's throne are raised slightly above the level of the feet of the supporting figures, who represent the lands of the empire. (Donald N. Wilber)

they appear to be ill suited as places in which eternal fires burned, hence the belief that they had other functions. It has been suggested, without clear evidence, that there was an ayadana on the Persepolis platform. Without being able to solve this problem of the function of the ayadana, it should be noted that the sacred fire probably burned on heights where it was visible for long distances, thus providing the prototype for the Sassanian practice of maintaining a chain of sacred fires on high places (the Sassanian dynasty ruled Iran from the third into the seventh century A.D.).

Haoma played a very important role in the ritual life of the older Aryans. It is thought that haoma produced a state of euphoria, but, except that it was obtained by pounding the twigs of a plant, nothing is known for certain about it. A Belgian scholar, Jacques Duchesne-Guillemin, has suggested that haoma was derived from ephedra, a plant common to Asia. The extract, obtained by pounding the twigs of the plant in a mortar, was ephedrine, an alkaloid. In pure states alkaloids are bitter tasting and comprise the stimulants in such substances as coffee, tea, tobacco, and opium. In the rituals haoma was mixed with milk, possibly to disguise its taste.

Just how haoma acted as a stimulant is unknown, but the evidence that its use continued into the Achaemenid period is convincing. Cylinder seals of the period show an altar on which rests the mortar and pestle used for the preparation of haoma. Tablets from the Treasury at Parsa name priests whose duty it was to prepare haoma, while the structure itself yielded a goodly number of mortars and pestles that were certainly used in its preparation. Herodotus wrote that the Persians made important decisions only after they had drunk deeply of wine; possibly he should have said that they made decisions under the influence of haoma.

In the excavations of Parsa a trilingual inscription of Xerxes, which had been engraved on three sides of a stone, was found. It has become known as the *daiva* inscription. Xerxes lists the lands of which he was king and then states: "And among these countries there was a (place) where previously false gods [daiva] were worshiped. Afterward, by the favor of Ahuramazda, I destroyed that sanctuary of the demons [daivadana], and I made a proclamation, 'The demons shall not be worshiped!' Where previously the demons were worshiped, there I worshiped Ahuramazda and Arta reverently."

The usual suggestion associated with this inscription, that Xerxes had come out strongly against the worship of the old Aryan gods, seems less convincing than one which ties it in with a historical event. Early in his reign Babylon

Bas-reliefs from Throne Hall. Ruler is seated above five tiers of soldiers. (Persian Gulf Command)

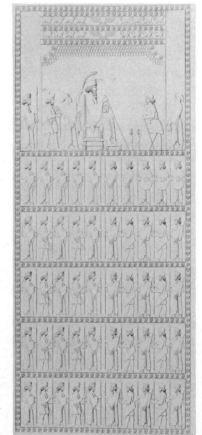

Nineteenth-century engraving of bas-relief with canopy over ruler's head. The winged disks on the canopy are symbols of the god Ahuramazda. (*Description de l'Arménie, la Perse, et la Mésopotamie*, by Charles Texier)

Door jamb panel from Throne Hall. Royal hero, in conflict with bull, drives a sword into the bull's stomach. (Iran Ministry of Information)

The Palace of Darius, showing the southern facade. The bas-reliefs are reminiscent of those on the apadana: guards facing a central panel and the conflict between the lion and bull filling the corner angles. (Iran National Tourist Organization)

revolted; Xerxes quickly visited a terrible punishment on it. Among other destruction, the 18-foot-high gold statue of Bel Marduk, the god of the city, was removed and melted down. Thus, the sanctuary of the demon who was responsible for the uprising was destroyed.

III

THE STRUCTURES
AT PARSA

The Platform

It is believed that Darius undertook the construction of Parsa about 520. One of his predecessors, Kurush (Cyrus II), had been an active builder at Pasargadae, where a gateway, small palaces, a fortified terrace, and his own tomb were strewn throughout a park-like area. Darius continued to build there, as is shown by the recovery of an inscription at the site. While the plans of these palaces were to find reflection at Parsa, the site of Parsa was a much bolder, more monumental concept.

Inscribed tablets found in the Treasury of Parsa indicate that construction went on for a very long time. Some of these tablets are dated to the initial campaign of work at the site under Darius and others continue through the first seven years of the Xerxes. Then there is a hiatus, with the tablets picking up in the nineteenth year of Xerxes and others dated through the fifth year of Artaxerxes I. Thus, these tablets suggest two separate, long periods of building activity.

The platform of Parsa was established from a terrace of natural rock that projects from the base of a rugged hillside at an altitude of 5,800 feet. As work was undertaken at the terrace, ravines and hollows were filled in by stones brought from adjacent quarries and by material obtained after leveling projecting spurs of rock. Care was given to making the best possible use of the natural levels of the terrace by establishing three finished surfaces at different heights. Along the three projecting sides of the terrace—some 1,400 feet from north to south and some 1,000 feet in depth from hillside to plain—the masons placed great blocks of limestone to form a massive retaining wall. Even before the retaining wall was completed, work could have gone forward on the platform, which rose as much as 50 feet above the plain.

Along the edges of the platform rose a high, thick wall of mud brick. The best preserved section of this wall, provided with projecting towers, is on the northeast area of the platform. There is a lack of agreement among students of the site as to whether or not this wall completely enclosed the platform: if it had, none of the structures on it would have been visible from the plain below, nor would people on the platform have been able to look out over the plain.

The unknown architect or engineer who supervised the work for Darius I is given credit for establishing a master plan for the many structures in advance of actual building. The principal evidence for this assumption is the presence of a series of underground channels intended to carry off the water that fell on the structures and the platform: the courses of these channels are in accord with the emplacement of structures built at later periods. Minor evidence for the preplanning of a single structure is the presence of limestone boxes containing gold and silver plates that were placed in cavities in the platform before the walls of the *apadana,* the audience hall of Darius, was erected above them.

Each succeeding structure was uniformly oriented with one axis aligned with the longest dimension of the platform, the north-south direction. Actually, this direction is south-southeast to north-northwest. Over many decades most of the platform was filled up, with successive structures fitted in alongside existing ones. Rather narrow passageways and corridors ran between the buildings, and numerous staircases provided access from level to level.

The stone masonry of Parsa displays very distinctive features. One might say that it looks as if it had been executed by carpenters and sculptors modeling in clay rather than by stone masons. For example, stones of relatively standard sizes are not to be found, nor are the jambs and lintels of doors and windows built of simple uprights and horizontal slabs. The masons made their job complicated by trying to "stretch" each block; examples of this method will be cited.

The quarries adjacent to the site apparently produced two types of blocks: first, there were very large monoliths, and, second, blocks of irregular sizes and shapes that may have been the pieces left over after the removal of the monoliths.

The blocks were quarried by a tedious but effective method. Deep grooves were cut with metal tools into the exposed rock surface and wooden wedges driven into them. The wedges were then soaked with water and as they swelled the rock was split away from its bed. Not only the four side faces of each block were established in this manner, but grooves and wedges were used below the block. Thus, the ancient quarry reflects where "bites" of stone were removed from it. The stone, a very hard limestone, contains bitumen and ranges in color from gray to brown to black.

Even before the blocks were removed from their beds iron tools came into play. Hammers with pointed ends and "points," or sharp pointed chisels, completed the process of separation and then were used for roughly dressing the surfaces of each block. This rough dressing might go quite far toward producing a finished piece: a column capital lying in a quarry is dressed to a close approximation of its finished shape.

After the blocks were moved onto the terrace proper they were finely dressed with flat-headed and toothed chisels, and, finally, carefully smoothed down with rasps and files. Throughout the terrace the bas-reliefs reflect the use of toothed chisels, and it has been convincingly argued that this tool was brought to Parsa by Greek masons between 520 and 515. The toothed chisel is believed to have been a Greek invention of the middle of the sixth century B.C. It was not used by the masons working at Pasargadae.

Finished pieces—column bases, column drums, and other elements—were carved with a variety of mason's marks before setting in place. Each such mark identified the output of a single gang of workmen and had meaning only to the workers and to their paymaster, since the marks were never on surfaces that were to be seen.

Some of the monoliths, such as the huge block 23 feet 6 inches long and 6 feet 7 inches high in the southern wall of the terrace that bears on its surface a trilingual inscription of Darius, were finished as almost perfect cubes; only the one face destined to go against the natural rock or against a mud brick wall was not finely dressed. Other monoliths were made into column drums or shaped at the building site to get as much out of each single block as possible. For example, some of the great slabs of the entrance stairway include both steps and a segment of the bounding parapet.

Blocks of irregular sizes and shapes were fitted together almost as the pieces of a jigsaw puzzle are assembled. The retaining walls of the entrance stairway best illustrate this technique: there are almost no continuous horizontal beds and relatively few vertical edges. The following method may have been used. At the wall the blocks were finely dressed on their front surface and on the

Detail of southern façade, the Palace of Darius. Carved figures of servants bearing food adorn the sides of the stairs. (Archaeological Service of Iran)

Palace of Darius, doorways to main hall and niches. The masonry was so highly polished that the room has aptly been called the Hall of Mirrors. (Persian Gulf Command)

base. As each block was moved into position, its roughly dressed ends were carefully dressed to fit snugly against adjacent blocks. Such finished edges might contain angles and even pockets, which were filled with smaller stones. Patching was prevalent not only on the walls of the platform but throughout the structures. Weak or damaged areas of stone were trimmed out and plugs inserted. Some such plugs are less than 2 inches in diameter. In addition, cramps were placed across the line of potential or actual breaks and cracks in the stones.

Throughout the walls of the platform and the structures the joints between adjacent stones are almost invisible. This effect, obtained by the extremely fine dressing of the blocks, was made more permanent by binding together adjacent stones with cramps of iron set into beds of lead. This technique helped to solidify the walls against the ravages of time and the effects of earthquakes (Parsa lies within a moderately active earthquake belt). In much later periods the iron and lead was pried out of the stones—the lead to make bullets and the iron to make weapons.

The work on the platform was never finished. One illustration of this fact is the presence of an area of protruding rock at the northwestern corner of the terrace that was never leveled off. While most of the people who have written about the site believe that it had only a single, monumental stairway from plain to platform, Erich Schmidt insisted that a service portal and staircase were situated at the southwest corner of the platform. The name of the monumental gateway, or portico, of Xerxes was "All Lands." Two tablets from the Treasury mention a gateway called All Prosperity, and it is reasonable to think that this was the service entrance to the platform, reserved for cooks, tradesmen, servants, guards, and slaves, and for the delivery of animals, beer, wine, clothing, arms, and all the other items required by those in residence. A location at the southeastern corner of the terrace would have necessitated only a short staircase, which would have come up right into the service and storage areas. Also, there is evidence of the existence of a gate and passageway at the northwestern corner.

How was the site provided with water for daily needs? A few writers seem to have confused the subsurface drainage system and its tunnels and channels with a water supply system. One may still see sections of a water conduit cut into the slope of the hillside just a few meters above the plain some distance to the north of the platform in the direction of the Pulvar River, but these limited sections are not adequate proof that a steady supply of running water came from the river to the site. Possibly the large cistern that was cut into the rocky

Palace of Darius. Attendant of
the ruler bearing ointment bot-
tle and towel. (Persian Gulf
Command)

hill just above the site was the major source of water for its inhabitants. There
is no trace whatsoever of a system of sanitary canals for the removal of human
waste from the platform nor, in the structures, any indication of latrines.

The history of Parsa was not that of many years of steady occupancy. At
first, of course, it was a vast builders' yard strewn with stones of all sizes and
peopled by hordes of workmen. Later, for another period of years, construction was suspended as the resources of the empire and the concern of the rulers
were diverted to foreign wars. In the later centuries of the dynasty the rulers
seem seldom to have been in residence at Parsa, and as a result, the structures
and the household utensils show no signs of usage and heavy wear. The art
and architecture of the platform was clearly the product of many styles and
influences, but the final product reflects a Persian genius for assimilation and
re-creation—a genius that was to mark the artistic output of all later periods
of the history of Iran.

A number of individuals have sought to identify the sources of the artistic
style and of the features of architectural construction and decoration at Parsa.
Naturally enough, they have tended to find such sources and influences within
the fields of their own special concentration. One scholar of broad interests

47

Elevation of the Triple Portal, showing bas-reliefs. The panels, intended for inscriptions, were left blank. (Persian Gulf Command)

finds Ionian influence in the bases and shafts of the columns; from Mesopotamia he derives the idea of the palaces on an artificial terrace, and from the same region the use of walls of mud brick decorated by carved slabs and glazed brick plaques and of gates guarded by winged bulls. He suggests that the portrayal of Ahuramazda as a bearded figure within a winged disk is a transferal of the manner in which the god Assur was shown on Assyrian palaces. In the lower sections of the column capitals he finds Egyptian influence and features from the eastern Mediterranean region, while he subscribes to the theory of the presence of Greek sculptors at Parsa.

Quite recently a suggestion made tentatively some years earlier that the kingdom of Urartu represented a strong formative influence on Achaemenid art and architecture has been revived with enthusiasm. From Urartu is said to have come the cyclopean stone work of the terraces found in Iran at Masjid-i-Sulayman, Pasargadae, and Parsa, as well as the concept of the terrace in stone. Also, the plan form of the apadana, the motive of the stepped battlement, and the origin of the addorsed animal capitals are credited to this kingdom.

48

The kingdom of Urartu, centered at Lake Van, was at its height about 750. It was attacked and ravaged by the Assyrian king Sargon II (722–705) and may have been completely overrun by people moving in from the north about 590. Since there is such a considerable gap in time between the major activity at Urartu and that at Parsa, the possibility of significant influence on Parsa seems doubtful.

Although few structures of the Median period remain, it is suggested that this architecture had a strong influence on the earliest Achaemenid building. This speculation will certainly be tested as new excavations in Iran bring to light Median sites, sites with buildings that are expected to look much like those of Cyrus at Pasargadae.

The platform is attained by a monumental, double reversing stairway in two flights, with a total of 111 steps. Long ago visitors noted that the steps were so wide and low that horses easily could be ridden up the stairway. The stairs are 23 feet wide, with treads of 12 inches and risers 4 inches high. As many as five of these steps and the flanking parapet were cut from a single monolith, 23 by 5 by 2 feet in size. Preserved sections of the parapet display the stepped battlement that occurs on several of the structures of Parsa.

Darius constructed the platform proper, the monumental stairway, the Triple Portal, and his private palace. He also carried out the first two building periods of the Treasury and began the apadana. Xerxes completed the apadana, built the gateway, or portico, called All Lands, his own palace and the so-called harem, and began the Throne Hall. Artaxerxes I completed the Throne Hall and began work on an unfinished portico that precedes it. He may have constructed a private palace; the remains are inconclusive.

The description of the buildings on the platform begins with the entrance gateway, moves to each of the two great columnar halls, then to the palaces of the rulers, and, finally, to those structures that served other functions.

Gateway All Lands

Just back from the head of the monumental stairway rises the fairly well preserved gateway named in its inscriptions as the "covered door All Lands" (B on the plan). Facing the stairway appear colossal figures of winged bulls whose forequarters project forward from massive piles of masonry. Similar figures adorn the opposite side of the structure, and above the four bulls are identical trilingual inscriptions, each twenty-four lines long. They read: "I am Xerxes, the great King, King of Kings, King of the lands of many peoples, king

Persians ascending the main staircase, the Triple Portal. Unlike the apadana stairs, which portray guards exclusively, the Triple Portal also depicts dignitaries of the realm. (Archaeological Service of Iran)

Detail of Persians on main staircase, the Triple Portal. (Iran National Tourist Organization)

of this great earth far and wide. By Ahuramazda's favor I made this covered door All Lands. Much that is beautiful has been built in this Parsa which I and my father have built. What now has been built and appears beautiful, all that we have built by the favor of Ahuramazda."

There were also later inscriptions. As Sir Ker Porter, writing in 1818, noted, "On both [sides], I am sorry to say, I found a cloud of initials, and names, and dates, of former visitants to the site, to the no small injury of the fine surface of the stone."

The structure is a chamber some 82 feet square; its roof was originally supported by four columns. Stone benches around its walls may have been provided for guards or for those waiting to be summoned to one of the structures on the platform. The colossal figures to the east differ from those on the west in having human heads rather than bulls' heads. The features of the four colossal figures were deliberately damaged by iconoclasts of the Islamic period to whom the representation of living forms was anathema. With their very long, square-cut beards, crowns, and slightly upcurving wings, these figures come directly from the Assyrian tradition. In fact, those on the east side of the structure display a striking resemblance to a winged, human-headed bull from the palace of King Sargon, 722–705, at Khorsabad, now in the museum of the Oriental Institute of the University of Chicago.

The presence of doors on the south and east of the chamber indicates that the gateway was designed to give access both to the apadana and to the Throne Hall. Its doors of wood must have been some 40 feet high and were certainly plated with metal; possibly only the lower part of these huge doors actually opened, like the small doors set into the large doors of cathedrals.

To the north of the gateway is a curious area, curious in that there is a natural outcropping of rock that was never leveled off to a flat surface as was the entire rest of the platform. In this area there are three stones that may mark the line of a passageway from an entrance gate. A central, flat stone is flanked on either side by an L-shaped block, with the possibility that the mud brick walls of the passageway rose from the uprights of the L's. In this area the level of the outcropping is the same height as the top of a quarry just to the north, and it would seem probable that most of the roughly dressed blocks came to the structures in which they were to be used through this area. For example, here is a very large column drum with a large crack; it was once repaired by a series of cramps across the crack, but seems to have been abandoned, possibly because of doubts as to its real soundness.

Just to the south and left of the gateway All Lands is a stone basin, certainly

Detail of Persians, the Triple Portal. Long covered by debris, the figures on the stairs are well preserved. (Iran National Tourist Organization)

for ceremonial ablutions. Carved from one immense block of stone, more than 6 feet square and 6 feet high, the basin related to an arm of the main drainage system of the platform.

The Apadana

To the south are the ruins of the apadana (C on the plan), raised on a ledge of rock that is about 8 feet 6 inches above the level of the gateway All Lands.

The apadana was probably under construction for some thirty years, as evidenced by glazed bricks with inscriptions of Xerxes found in the excavations. While the visitor is initially impressed by the ranks of tall columns, attention quickly shifts to its two staircases: one on the north of the hall and one to the east. The staircase on the north was never completely covered by debris and blown dust and hence was looted by tourists and treasure seekers; a number of its stones are in museums and private collections. Since the stairway on the east was entirely concealed by earth until its excavation in 1932, it is much better preserved.

The faces of the figures of the north stairway were badly mutilated by successive generations of Muslims. Ker Porter aptly described this wanton destruction: ". . . the whole of his face is gone, having left only the beard . . . the dress of this man, and his five followers, is exactly alike; and all sharing the same progress, more or less, towards decapitation." This mutilation extends throughout the platform, and includes the visages of animals.

The stairways depict representatives of the lands of the empire bringing tribute to the great king. There are the same number of groups of the same peoples on each façade, and they are portrayed as if seen from opposite sides; that is, as if they were filing between two lines of guards with the guards in one line seeing them from one side and the guards in the other line from the other side. The north stair was the first to be executed, certainly during the reign of Darius. However, no inscriptions were carved by him on any of the three panels prepared for that purpose. The central panel is blank, as is the panel at the eastern end, while the western panel contains an inscription of Xerxes stating that all which he had built here and elsewhere was through the favor of Ahuramazda. The text is known as XPb. All Achaemenid inscriptions in Old Persian of any significant length are given in transliteration and translation in Roland G. Kent, *Old Persian: Grammar, Texts, Lexicon*, where they are identified by ruler, place, and by the number executed under a ruler. Thus, XPb equals Xerxes, Persepolis, inscription b. The central panel of the east stairway is also blank. The panel on its southern end has an inscription almost identical with that of Xerxes already mentioned, while the panel at the northern end contains the Elamite and Akkadian versions of the Old Persian inscription. No explanation can be offered as to why the conspicuous central panels of both stairways were never inscribed.

Each of the stairways has two sets of staircases: a central section, with its flights of steps, which abut against the long facade of the stairways, and flights of steps at the extreme ends of the facades. The facades of the stairways depict a carefully staged procession that took place at the New Year's festival. As it is shown, this procession had ascended the monumental entrance stairway and passed through the gateway All Lands to assemble in the open area before the apadana, hemmed in between long lines of guards.

The façades that bear the apadana reliefs are made up of monolithic slabs of varying length, some of them more than twelve feet long. For the east stairway those slabs placed directly on the living rock of the terrace include the two lower registers of the tributary groups and nearly half of the upper register. The second, higher, row of slabs includes the top of the upper register and the projecting stepped battlements; their vertical joints do not line up with those of the base slabs.

As mentioned previously, there was an apparent compulsion to quarry and make use of the largest possible pieces of stone. What may be regarded as normal masonry practice would have been to standardize sizes of blocks and to establish horizontal joints in relationship with the general design, that is, at the top of the second register rather than in the middle of the upper register. Also, in so-called normal practice the panels destined for inscriptions would have been separate slabs of stone; here, however, one panel slab contains part of a tributary group, while another is cut by a vertical joint. In defense of the special technique employed, it may be said that the joints were so carefully fitted as to have been invisible once the façades were completed. It is certain that the slabs were moved into final position with perfectly finished horizontal (top and bottom) and vertical (side) faces and with undressed front faces. The fact that the stepped battlements project forward several inches from the finished face of the upper register is proof that the front faces were fine dressed in place.

The central staircase of the eastern stairway was never quite finished: a number of the rosettes of the bounding frames were never executed and a part of the relief below the stepped battlements was not completed. Similar unfinished areas occur throughout the structures—perhaps the inspectors responsible for checking details failed to do their duty.

The identification of the lands from which the twenty-three tributary groups came derives from two major sources: Achaemenid inscriptions that list these lands and the representation of similarly clad figures in reliefs that show these individuals upholding royal thrones.

The Behistun inscription of Darius (DB) and that of Darius on the southern retaining wall of Parsa (DPe) both list twenty-three lands. An inscription of

Darius at Susa (DSe) lists twenty-nine lands, while an inscription of Xerxes at Parsa (XPh) gives thirty-one lands.

The posthumous tomb of Darius at Naqsh-i-Rustam depicts thirty throne upholders, who are identified (DNa). On the tomb assigned to Artaxerxes II the throne upholders are identified by country in short trilingual inscriptions relating to each figure.

Another useful source is Herodotus, who in one passage lists twenty satrapies of Darius and in another names and gives descriptions of the costumes and weapons of many of the some thirty-eight nations that made up the armies of Xerxes. R. D. Barnett also made comparisons between the clothing and accouterments of the figures from the stairways with representations of similar figures on objects of art contemporary in date, but from other regions. The bas-reliefs were probably executed either between 510 and 500 or shortly after 500.

Although panels on both stairways bear inscriptions of Xerxes, these texts make no mention of the apadana itself. Possibly the structure of the apadana was completed first, then the north stairway, and, finally, the east stairway was built under Xerxes. Evidence for this assumption is present. In 1967 trenches were dug behind the façade wall of the east stair preparatory to installing a concrete backing that would prevent moisture from soaking up into the reliefs. These trenches revealed well-constructed courses of masonry below the level of the apadana floor, and it appears that these courses marked the east side of the apadana as it was completed under Darius and that the east stairway itself was a later addition. Alternately, Xerxes completed the apadana and added the east stairway later. Still on the subject of evidence, a comparison of the compositions of like delegations on the two stairways clearly indicates that the east stair reflects a refinement over the northern one in such features as spacing and number of figures.

The building is not called the apadana in any existing inscription. It is assumed that its immediate prototype was the apadana of Darius at Susa, although the undated inscriptions at Susa do not prove the priority of that building. The apadana, "palace," at Susa was built by Darius adjacent to his *hadish*, which was destroyed by fire in the reign of Artaxerxes I and rebuilt by Artaxerxes II, according to A²Sa. The correct name of the Parsa structure may have been "columnar hall," which appears as *i-ia-an* and *hi-ia-an-na* on two tablets from the Treasury that are assigned to the reign of Darius.

The plans and details of the structures at Susa and Parsa are very similar.

Median dignitaries ascending the stairway, the Triple Portal. The requirements of isocephaly resulted in a mixture of dwarfs and giants. (Archaeological Service of Iran)

Informally portrayed, the Medes march along by ones and by twos on the Triple Portal stairway. Some turn to look at those behind them; one extends a helping hand. (Archaeological Service of Iran)

Each had its great hall with thirty-six columns and its columnar porticoes. The columns rose from bell-shaped bases and carried double-bull capitals above vertical volutes (volutes are the spiral-shaped forms found also in the Ionic capitals of the Greeks). At Parsa experiments were conducted with double-eagle and double-lion capitals on the columns of at least one of the porticoes.

The great hall of the apadana at Parsa is some 197 feet square and its columns, with their capitals, rose to a height of 65 feet. Including those of the porticoes, there were seventy-two columns. In 1621 Pietro della Valle recorded that twenty-five of the columns were still standing, while in 1828 an observer saw only thirteen, the number standing today.

Beneath the base courses of the walls, in the northeast and the southeast corners, the excavators unearthed two stone boxes. Each box contained a thick sheet of gold and one of silver that bear trilingual inscriptions of Darius defining the extent of his reign. They read, "This is the kingdom which I hold. From the Sakae beyond Sogdiana to Ethiopia, from India to Sardis, which Ahura-mazda, greatest of the gods, presented me."

Although the hall could have held up to ten thousand people, it was not well suited for permitting large numbers to see the ruler in splendor on his throne. The columns were relatively slender in proportion to their height, but there were so many that they effectively interfered with the view of any single point, such as the place of the throne, except for those in the central aisle and the aisle at right angle to the throne.

Perhaps there was a deliberate effort to keep the ruler from being too directly observed. If so, the architecture of the hall certainly served to preserve his remoteness. The interior of the structure must have been very dark; since little daylight could have come through the portals, flaming torches must have provided illumination.

It has been suggested that the walls of the central hall rose above the roofs of the porticoes and were pierced with windows, providing so-called clerestory lighting for the interior. However, since the walls of the hall were of mud brick, it would not have been possible to make openings of any size and number in these walls without endangering their strength, and this strength had to be maintained in order to hold up the roof beams of the hall. Also, the fact that the columns of the hall and of the porticoes had the same diameters presumes that the columns were all of the same height and hence all the roofs of the same height. Some light may have come through glass globes set in the roof, a practice common in present-day Iran.

The system of constructing and roofing the apadana was also employed for

Median dignitaries, the Triple Portal. Nearly all carry flowers, which they sniff with pleasure. (Archaeological Service of Iran)

Triple Portal. Detail of Medes on main staircase. (Iran National Tourist Organization)

all the other structures on the platform. The first stage in construction was to raise the columns in place on their bases and crown them with the huge capitals. These columns were set on bell-shaped bases decorated with stylized floral designs; the shafts had between forty and forty-eight flutes. At the top of the shaft the lowest element of the composite capital was a ring of drooping sepals. Above it was a crowning motive similar to the palm leaf capitals of Egypt, with each segment decorated with a carved papyrus flower. Then came an elongated section with pairs of vertical double volutes, and finally, the impost block with its doubled animal forequarters.

To raise the columns and place the capitals on them a combination of earth ramps, timber scaffolds, and tall wood frames holding ropes and pulleys must have been used. Once the columns and capitals were in place the scaffolds and ramps were taken away. Next the portal and window jambs and lintels of dressed stone were put into place, their exterior sides and upper surfaces only roughly dressed. The spaces between and above the masonry-lined apertures were filled with mud (sun dried) brick walls—more than 17 feet thick.

In building the walls, the bricklayers may well have followed the method used in Iran today, that of standing on the walls that rose beneath them as they laid down successive courses of bricks. The "up-carriers" mentioned in the Treasury tablets brought the bricks and the semiliquid mud mortar to the site. The bricks were probably tossed from level to level, from hand to hand, until they reached the bricklayers, who placed them on beds of mortar. The bricks of the apadana walls are about 13 inches square and more than 5 inches thick.

When the walls attained the height of the column capitals, they were smoothly topped with baked brick or fired tiles to establish a level bearing surface. Next, great roof beams, square in section, were drawn up to the top of the walls by ropes. How long these beams were is unknown, but it is not too difficult to establish the lengths required to cover the hall with the fewest possible timbers of manageable lengths. First a timber some 64 feet long was so maneuvered that one end slid through the U-shaped saddle of the first capital from the wall and came to rest with that end halfway through the middle of the next capital. With the other end resting on half the width of the wall, it spanned two of the seven aisles of the hall. This process was continued until six beams were in place, and then it was repeated at the opposite side of the hall. This left the three center aisles to be bridged; this bridging could have been done with six timbers, each over 84 feet in length, or with twelve shorter timbers.

Triple Portal. Median dignitary, bearing large fruit. (Iran National Tourist Organization)

Persian and Median guards, Triple Portal. Unlike the dignitaries, these figures are formally portrayed, with spears resting on the forward foot. (Iran National Tourist Organization)

Over the grid formed by the main roof beams a cross grid of lighter timbers was placed and fastened to the ones below by wooden pegs. I Kings 7:2–4, which are among the many verses describing the "house of the forest of Lebanon" built by Solomon, appear to reflect the use of cedar beams to form a major grid and a secondary cross grid. Over the cross grid were laid smaller planks or poles, then straw mats, and, finally, a layer of mixed gravel and soil. This exposed surface was waterproof provided its upkeep was not neglected. As is done today, stone rollers were probably used to pack down fresh layers of gravel and soil at intervals. Rain (snow is quite rare at Parsa) was either led down drains built into the walls that connected with the underground channels or led out spouts of such length that the falling water did not splash against the lower walls.

The exterior and interior surfaces of the mud brick walls were extensively decorated. At Susa some of the exterior walls were lined with glazed bricks; numerous pieces of similar bricks that were found in front of the apadana have been reassembled in a panel now in the Archaeology Museum in Tehran. Fragments of various kinds from the excavations suggest that all interior walls had a base coating of mud plaster about 2 inches thick and over it a thin wash of greenish-gray plaster. The dado level, that of the lower walls, may have been decorated with designs in color.

Above the dado level hangings may well have covered all the walls. The Book of Esther records a feast held in the court of the king's palace at Shushan (Susa): "There were hangings of white cloth, of green and of blue, fastened with cords of fine linen and purple . . ." This same passage speaks of "a pavement of red, and white, and yellow, and black marble," but no fragments of marble flooring were recovered from the apadana. Instead, a wash of greengray plaster covered the floor. (In the so-called harem, floors were colored red.)

According to an inscription of Artaxerxes II, the palace of Darius at Susa was destroyed by fire. With inflammable hangings and wooden roofs fire must also have been a great hazard at Parsa. The grids of the roof beams were certainly decorated with painted and carved designs, although such decoration would scarcely have been visible from the floor of the dimly lit hall.

The double leaf doors of the portals did not swing on hinges. Instead, into the side, or edge, of each leaf that came up against the stone jamb a circular, vertical wood post was inset; this post turned freely in a stone socket. The wooden doors were plated with thin sheets of bronze and of precious metals with designs in relief. Fragments of such sheets were found by excavators,

Triple Portal. Head of Persian guard. (Iran National Tourist Organization)

Hand of guard, the Triple Portal. Fingers and nails were finely executed with toothed chisels, then buffed to a high sheen with abrasive stones. (Iran National Tourist Organization)

while dealers in antiquities in countries other than Iran display very large bronze plaques.

A problem related to the appearance and function of the apadana concerns what went on in the area of its west portico. According to some recent speculation, there was a break in the enclosing wall along the edge of the platform just at this section so that the ruler, seated on a portable throne, could view the plain below. More will be said about the questions related to the wall that enclosed the platform area at a later point.

Throne Hall

The Throne Hall (K on the plan) was long called the Hall of One Hundred Columns. From the east portal of the gateway All Lands, a processional way led between mud brick walls. That this way was lined at intervals with sculptured figures is suggested by the unfinished statue of a dog sitting on its haunches that was found in this area and is now in the museum at the site, together with a similar completed piece now on display in the Archaeological Museum in Tehran.

This passageway continued beyond an unfinished gateway to turn into secondary corridors giving access to minor structures. This gateway, begun by Artaxerxes I and possibly never completed, had a central square chamber with four columns and long, narrow rooms on its eastern and western sides. From its southern doorway one entered a large open court in front of the Throne Hall, while to the east and west this court was bounded by mud brick walls and other buildings.

The façade of the Throne Hall presented a central porch with two rows of eight columns flanked by masonry *antae*, or end walls, with figures of colossal bulls. Large fragments of these bulls were found by excavators and are now being assembled. The hall itself was 225 feet square; its roof was supported by ten rows of ten columns each. These columns were more slender than those of the apadana and rose to a height of 37 feet, less than half the height of the apadana columns. There were two portals in each of the four sides of the hall and between the portals a series of masonry niches or reveals. As in the apadana, mud brick filled the spaces between the masonry elements and comprised the upper walls. A foundation record on stone that was uncovered in the hall states that Xerxes began construction and Artaxerxes I completed it.

The jambs of the portals on the northern and southern sides of the hall show the ruler Artaxerxes I in audience, enthroned beneath a canopy and a winged

The winged symbol of the god Ahuramazda, as represented on a doorway of the main hall, the Triple Portal. (Oriental Institute, University of Chicago)

disk, with dignitaries before him and attendants standing behind the throne. On the northern portals five tiers of guards are portrayed, while on the south the ruler's throne is upheld by representatives of twenty-eight lands.

In these reliefs and those from other structures that portray the ruler upheld on his throne, the legs of the thrones are raised slightly above the level on which the lowest line of supporting figures stand. On the reliefs of the royal tombs the fact that the throne has been lifted off the ground is more apparent. The significance of these scenes is clear: on ceremonial occasions the rulers were borne on their thrones from relatively private quarters to places of appearance or audience.

The figure of Ahuramazda is seen hovering over the ruler on the side portals, but there are no representations of Anahita or Mithra. On the jambs of the eastern and western portals, the royal hero drives a short sword into the bellies of such beasts as a bull, a lion, a winged lion with a bird's claw, and a mythical animal with a lion's head and the tail of a scorpion—beasts that might appear after indulging in too much haoma.

Unlike the apadana, which had stately porticoes on three sides of its great hall, the Throne Hall had only the northern porch, with the portals on the other three sides of the hall opening into very narrow, flanking corridors. Erich Schmidt, its excavator, named it the Throne Hall after the reliefs showing the ruler enthroned and suggested that it had the additional function of displaying, near the throne, a selection of precious objects from the Treasury. This theory has not been authenticated, but it is reasonable to believe that the Throne Hall did not serve the same purposes as did the apadana. Another theory, proposed by André Godard, formerly head of the Archaeological Service of Iran, is that the structure was a hall of honor, or of reunion, of the Achaemenid army. He points out that the reliefs in the buildings show the ruler's throne being upheld by five tiers of soldiers as representatives of that army, and that just to the east of the hall were the quarters of the military garrison of Parsa. Thus, according to Godard, the renowned Immortals assembled in this hall annually, if not more frequently. This theory, too, is unsupported by factual data and does not correspond with the identification of Parsa as the site of the New Year's festival.

Palace of Darius

The southernmost section of the apadana, which matched in size the open porticoes on the other three sides of the hall, was subdivided into a maze-like series of rooms. There was access, however, from this section to the palace of Darius, situated on the highest level of the platform. However, since that palace faced south, one came up against its blank rear wall and either had to go around a corner to a flight of stairs on its western side or as far as the southern façade with its stairways.

The palace of Darius (I on the plan) has been called the *tachara* by all who have written about the site. It is so named, as *tacara*, in the inscriptions of Darius on the walls. It has been suggested that a tachara was a private palace, a little "paradise" for a ruler. Hadish seems to have been the generic term for palace: when Xerxes added inscriptions to this same tachara, he called it a hadish. As one faces its southern façade, the treatment of its plinth or base is reminiscent of the central, projecting elements of the stairways of the apadana.

65

The same lines of guards face a central panel, and the conflict of lion and bull fills in the corner angles. A new note is present: the side walls of the stairs bear carved figures of servants carrying food into the palace.

The portico with its two rows of four columns was flanked at either end by a tall monolithic shaft (one shaft has fallen) and cuttings near their tops were certainly intended to take the ends of the roof beams of the portico. Around the three sides of the portico, windows and blind niches alternate. Figures of guards are carved on the jambs of its side portals, which opened into small rooms.

The central door of the portico gave access to the main hall of the palace. Its jambs bear relief figures of the ruler, who is shown sheltered by a parasol held by an attendant. The figure on the right jamb once bore the name Darius in three languages on a fold of its garment; this inscription was fairly neatly chiseled off and found its way to the Cabinet des Médailles, Bibliothèque Nationale, Paris. To the figure on the opposite jamb the name of Xerxes was added in Old Persian and Elamite.

It is usually said that Xerxes completed this palace. He did order inscriptions carved on the monolithic shafts and on the southern wall; they (inscriptions XPca, XPcb, and XPcc) state that the hadish was built by Darius and ask protection of Ahuramazda for "what was built by me, and what was built by my father Darius the King."

The main hall of the palace displays the bases, which held three rows of four columns each; portals lead to rooms on three sides. On the jamb of the door to the east the ruler stabs a rampant lion, and on the two doors to the west he subdues both a composite beast and a bull. On the cornices of the windows and niches of this hall are identical inscriptions in Old Persian, repeated eighteen times and reading, "stone window frames, made in the house of King Darius." All this masonry was so highly polished that the room has been aptly called the Hall of Mirrors. Its smooth surfaces together with the fact that the elements remained exposed above ground attracted later visitors to record statements in Pahlavi, Arabic, and Persian. The moldings of this palace include the cavetto, or concave, cornices over the doorways that are very Egyptian in style; probably it was here that the Egyptians brought to "execute inscriptions" worked.

To the north of the main hall two doors led into additional chambers, and the intimate character of these rooms is suggested by the nature of the reliefs on the door jambs. On one a youthful attendant carries a perfume or ointment jar and a folded towel; on the other jamb an attendant bears a brazier and a vessel. Other jambs depict the ruler holding a scepter and a flower, followed by attendants with a towel and a fly whisk made of a bull's tail. On the west side of the structure is a stairway erected, according to its inscription, by Artaxerxes III.

The tachara may have had more the function of a banquet hall than a private residence, and the small number of rooms supports this view. Possibly the ruler himself was the sole occupant of the palace on a limited number of occasions, with his consorts, courtiers, and attendants housed elsewhere.

In one of his inscriptions on the south wall of the platform, Darius calls the site a "fortress," and he may have found his world within its walls. The porch of the tachara opens on a level area of some size in which no traces of construction remain. A garden may have occupied this area. The presence of windows looking from the main hall out through the portico has given rise to the idea that the ruler could enjoy from there the view over the plain beyond. This idea is in contradiction to the long held belief that the entire platform was enclosed within a very high mud brick wall, and sections of this wall were found. Some of those who subscribe to this belief looked for loopholes, or rather breaks, in this wall. For example, one such break would have been to the south of the tachara; another break, adjacent to the west portico of the apadana, near the grand staircase, would have permitted the ruler to survey the plain and the settlement beyond. In opposition to these suggestions, it may be said that the desire to view and to enjoy the beauty of ever-changing nature is essentially a modern concept, one not necessarily held by the people of ancient times.

Triple Portal

Easily accessible from the eastern staircase of the apadana—just a short distance to the south—is a structure whose original purpose is not known. It has been variously called the Council Hall, Central Hall, Tripylon, Triple Portal (E on the plan), and, more recently, the King's Gate. This last name was suggested because the structure was so located that a ruler could go from it to any other part of the platform. The present writer prefers Triple Portal, a name that reflects the basic plan of the structure and avoids any personal notions as to its possible functions.

The panels on the stairs of the Triple Portal, which should have contained inscriptions, were left blank. It has been suggested that the Triple Portal was a hall of council, where high officials met with the ruler. Another suggestion is that it was used for banquets. Although the plan of the structure seems

Column capital from the Triple Portal, now in the Archaeological Museum, Tehran. (Archaeological Service of Iran)

unsuitable for large scale dining, such use is suggested by the reliefs on the sides of a very small staircase on the southern edge of the structure. Servants, dressed in robes or tunics, are shown carrying items for a feast, although not all of them are ready to serve. One figure carries a lamb, another a kid, and others a wineskin, drinks already poured into bowls, and food kept warm by holding a cover tightly over its container. Banquets were certainly held at Parsa, and such feasts can be reconstructed—not here—from the accounts in the Book of Esther and in Herodotus.

The Palace of Xerxes

The hadish of Xerxes (F on the plan) is to the south of the Triple Portal and the tachara of Darius and was at the highest level of the platform. Considerably larger than the palace of Darius, it was essentially an expanded version of the same plan. For example, its central hall had six rows of six columns each rather than multiples of four as in the structure of Darius.

It is much less well preserved than the tachara of Darius. As could be expected, the details are much like those of the earlier palace, as, for example, in the scene of the ruler under the parasol. A number of trilingual inscriptions repeat much the same information, such as XPda, XPdb, XPea, and XPeb. In each one Xerxes carefully relates himself to his father and states that "by the favor of Ahuramazda, this hadish I built." Since Xerxes also relates himself to Darius in his father's palace it is difficult to understand why he failed to extend this sense of recognition and of close relationship with Darius to the blank panels of the apadana stairways.

The inner surfaces of the window frames have reliefs depicting attendants carrying food and leading ibexes. The door jambs of the portals leading from the main hall to the smaller rooms have bas-reliefs very like in character to those similarly placed in the tachara of Darius; attendants carry an incense burner, a pail, and a towel.

Placed on the highest level of the platform, hence most exposed to the elements and to looters, the palace is poorly preserved and offers nothing significantly different in design and decoration from other structures to retain our attention.

Other Structures

Three structures, usually referred to as D, G, and H, are in the same general area of the platform as the palaces of Darius and Xerxes. These structures are either badly ruined or unexcavated.

Structure D revealed very little to the excavators, and its stones may have been systematically removed. Its portico faced north on an open court. On the opposite side of this court was the Triple Portal, while on its west side a portico and stairs led to the court in front of the palace of Xerxes. One recent writer states, without any evidence, that this building was a banquet hall for army officers.

Structure G is now but a mound of earth and fragments of stone. It has even been asserted that there never was a building on the site, that it was merely a place for depositing debris. Another supposition is that there was an open air shrine or temple, which had two or three superimposed terraces and towered over the roofs of the adjacent palaces. Later on, according to this theory, the facades of these terraces collapsed and the debris was removed by Darius III. Both these ideas seem unconvincing. Visible on the side of the mound toward the apadana are the lower courses of a flight of steps and also a vertical cutting against the natural rock face. It seems strange that the excavators have neglected this mound. As early as 1891, W. H. Blundell, who dug briefly at the site, sank some trenches into this mound, which he thought was the most fruitful place for excavations of any part of the platform.

Structure H lies to the east of the palace of Xerxes. Originally thought to be the palace of Artaxerxes III, the excavators determined that it had been put together from stones robbed from other buildings on the terrace and that it was probably not finished. Its plan is asymmetrical, unlike all the other buildings of this area, and the excavators concluded that it was assembled after the destruction of the site but prior to the Islamic period. Possibly it stands on the site of a palace of Artaxerxes I.

All the other buildings of Parsa served for purposes of administration, storage, and to house its garrison. Among these structures of a considerable variety of plan types are included the so-called Treasury, identified on the plan as L. This name may be accepted for an extensive complex of rooms while realizing that treasures were also stored in other areas.

The Treasury

The Treasury was originally constructed by Darius, then enlarged by him, and made still more spacious by Xerxes. The first rather small structure was expanded by the addition of an open rectangular courtyard with rooms ranged about it. Throughout this area, slender wood columns on stone bases were used, while the lower courses of the original walls have been rebuilt and crowned with a protective coping of baked tiles.

To the north and to the south, the porticoes that fronted on the courtyard had roofs supported by rows of wooden columns, while the rear walls of the eastern and southern porticoes displayed splendid life-size reliefs of Darius and his successor, Xerxes, each more than 20 feet long. The relief on the south, the better preserved, was removed to the Archaeological Museum in Tehran.

The expansion of the complex under Darius included a large hall to the west of the courtyard with nine rows of eleven columns each. The additions of Xerxes included a hall on the north side of the area; it had five rows of twenty columns each and hence was of impressive size. In both these large halls, wooden columns stood on discoid tori, each set on a square stone plinth. These stone elements bear a great variety of masons' marks, but none of these marks are of such a nature, as, for example, letter forms, as to suggest the nationality of the stonecutters.

It seems quite probable that the so-called Treasury was the first structure to be completed on the platform. Then, as work was going ahead on the apadana, the palace of Darius, and the Triple Portal, it fulfilled at least three functions. First, it was a hall of royal audience, as the twin bas-reliefs indicate. Second, it was the administrative office of the site, and, third, it housed the paraphernalia of the court as well as its treasures.

The excavation of the Treasury, with its nearly one hundred rooms, halls, and alcoves, revealed that it had been looted and many objects wantonly destroyed prior to its burning. The objects left behind by the looters included items too small to be easily noticed, and others that may have been smashed to bits because they had no negotiable value.

The Treasury housed not only precious metal and clothing and furniture, but also objects of pre-Achaemenid times assembled from conquered shrines, palaces, and cities. Some of the pieces left behind by the looters were inscribed with the names of pharaohs of Egypt, monarchs of Assyria and Babylonia, and, in a single example, a Hittite ruler.

An alabaster bowl bears the cartouches of the pharaoh Necho, and other objects of alabaster carry the name of the pharaoh Amasis. A drinking vessel of black and white granite, with four lions as handles, has the name Ashurbanipal. This vessel could have been taken by the Medes when they captured Nineveh in 612, next deposited at Ecbatana, and then taken by the Achaemenids, first to Pasargadae and then to Parsa. The torso of a seated female figure, clad in a clinging garment and executed in Greece at about the time of the Parthenon sculptures, is now in the Archaeological Museum in Tehran. Quantities of artistic treasures are known to have been brought from the Greek mainland. Xerxes had statues of Harmodius and Aristogeiton taken to Susa; they were found there by Alexander and sent back to Athens, where they were set up in the Acropolis. Coins antedating the foundation of Parsa were found, as well as cylinder seals carved centuries before the Achaemenid era.

Some twenty-three cylinder seals of the period of Parsa itself were recovered, a number of which offer different versions of scenes shown in the bas-reliefs of the structures. A ruler, so indicated by his robe, tiara, and long, square-cut beard, is victor over beasts that flank him. Priests conduct worship before an altar on which stands the mortar and pestle used to prepare haoma. The Ahuramazda symbol is attended by worshipers. Other seals and signet rings are clearly of Greek manufacture and may have been worn by Greeks attached to the royal court.

Quantities of what the excavators called royal tableware were found. Many bear the name of Xerxes in Old Persian, Elamite, Akkadian, and Egyptian. It has been suggested that many of them were broken as the looters stripped away the gold strips lining the rims or the gold liners of the vessels. There were plates, bottles, trays, and tripod bowls as well as fragments of glass and bronze vessels. Fragments of some three hundred ritual vessels were recovered. These were the mortars and pestles of chert, a hard green quartz, which were almost certainly used in the preparation of haoma. Objects of local manufacture in bronze were also found. Typical is an impressive bronze pedestal made up of three striding lions.

There were no traces of the more exotic objects that classical authors tell us were found at Parsa. These included golden plane trees and a golden vine that bore grapes of jewels.

The Harem

Just to the west of the Treasury is an extensive structure that Ernst Herzfeld, its initial excavator, labeled the harem, or women's quarters. This structure was said to have housed the many wives and the many more concubines of the rulers. While Greek sources make much of these companions of the kings, no Achaemenid documents mention them.

In his initial report on the site, Herzfeld stated that the tachara of Darius could easily be rebuilt to serve as the living quarters of excavators. Once active at the site, he chose to rebuild a considerable part of the so-called harem as the living quarters for his staff. Some years later these chambers were turned into a museum, now housing artifacts from Parsa and the surrounding region, although the most significant pieces found in the excavations at Parsa have been taken to the Archaeological Museum in Tehran.

This structure is approached from the north across an open courtyard and displays the restored portico and façade. The larger chambers show the characteristic construction of masonry portals and niches and mud brick walls. While there are a number of fairly large rooms, the plan features a series of very small chambers arranged along both sides of a narrow passageway; such rooms must have been very dark and gloomy. In fact, the present writer subscribes to the opinion that the so-called harem was a series of storerooms, additional to those of the Treasury. In support of this opinion is the fact that the excavations of this area failed to turn up a single article of personal adornment.

Storerooms and Military Quarters

Still farther to the west, in an area alongside and to the south of the palace of Xerxes, storerooms were excavated. Typical of these rooms is that each one had four columns, so indicated by the preserved bases. The columns were of wood, and stone members lined niches and doorways.

This same area, excavated only in very recent years, brought to light narrow chambers, with barrel vaults of mud brick. Because these chambers are located in the most easily defended part of the platform, it has been suggested that they may have contained the reserves of gold and silver talents.

The excavations also uncovered a series of rooms to the east of the Throne Hall. This area appears to have housed the soldiers of the garrison and to have included quarters for horses and chariots. This housing for men and beasts abutted against the hillside. The engineer in charge took the precaution of digging a wide, deep trench along this section, a trench adequate to carry off the water that poured down the slope of the Mount of Mercy after the rare torrential rains.

Just within this trench rose the enclosing wall, 33 to 39 feet thick and preserved in this section to some 40 feet of its assumed 60 feet of height. Portions of this wall along the north edge of the platform display towers at intervals and rooms within the towers. The so-called fortification tablets found in this area may have been moved from the Treasury to dead storage here when those accounts were no longer active.

A Settlement Below the Platform

Although only small areas have been excavated, a settlement on the plain below the platform seems to have been a sizable town with permanent residences for rulers and dignitaries. These structures had columns and portals of masonry and walls of mud brick. In 1952 a structure that had inscribed column

73

Detail of column capital from the Triple Portal. (Archaeological Service of Iran)

bases naming it the "tachara of Xerxes the king" was uncovered and an eagle-headed double capital was found. This tachara seems to have been set within a large garden, which had an ornamental lake, with the area bounded by a wall of the town. The remains of a larger edifice located closer to the platform may be those of a residential palace of Darius, although no inscriptions have as yet been recovered. Also, the extent of the excavations remains too limited to indicate whether these edifices housed servants as well as masters, or whether there were separate settlements or quarters for servants and slaves.

The Royal Tombs

The site later called Naqsh-i-Rustam—its Achaemenid name is unknown— was intimately related to Parsa. Into its cliff, six miles distant from Parsa, are carved the tombs of four Achaemenid rulers. As one faces the cliff they are, from left to right, believed to be those of Darius II, Artaxerxes I, Darius, and Xerxes. Only that of Darius bears inscriptions that name this ruler so that the assignment of the other tombs to later rulers represents merely informed speculation. It seems incredible that three of the rulers failed to carve their names on their own tombs, and it may be that the other tombs were not built by these kings.

The four tombs are similar in design. Each is in the form of a Greek cross with vertical and horizontal elements of almost equal length, deeply cut into the cliff, some 60 feet wide and 70 feet high. The horizontal bar of the cross is carved to resemble a portico, reflecting its original wood members. Four attached columns, crowned by bull capitals, support the horizontal beams of the entablature. The lower segment of the vertical bar is a smooth surface; the upper segment displays a two-story platform upheld by representatives of thirty lands. On the tomb of Darius these upholders were identified by labels, a few of which have survived.

On this platform are two stepped tiers: the ruler stands on one, and the other is crowned by a fire altar. Above this scene hovers the symbol of Ahuramazda. On the tomb of Darius twelve dignitaries watch the scene; they are crowded into vertical lines on both edges.

At the center of the façades of each tomb is a sculptured doorway; the molding of the doorway covers a larger area than the actual opening that leads into the interior chamber. Each chamber has a series of niches on either side, designed to receive the burials of the rulers and members of their immediate families.

In front of the tomb of Darius are traces of a mud brick wall that probably enclosed a sacred precinct. Within this enclosure stands the so-called Ka'ba-i-Zardusht, or Shrine of Zarathushtra, a replica of the much less well preserved Zandan-i-Sulayman, or Prison of Sulayman, at Pasargadae. There is no general agreement as to the purpose of the two structures. They may have been tombs, temples, or religious archives. If tombs, they would have housed the remains of the predecessors of Darius and of Cyrus. If they were fire temples, their plans are ill suited to contain the eternal flame.

Other rock-cut tombs situated closer to Parsa are believed to be those of other Achaemenid rulers. In the hillside above Parsa is a tomb ascribed to Artaxerxes II, because of the number of lands named in its inscriptions. These inscriptions copy some of those of the tomb of Darius; the labels of the up-holders are better preserved, but the name of a ruler is not present. To the southeast of Parsa is a tomb assigned to Artaxerxes III, and about a half mile to the south of the site is an unfinished tomb said to be that of Darius III. This latter tomb was at a poorly selected site. The lower part of the scene of worship of Ahuramazda is carved into the living rock, while the upper section was done into masonry blocks placed above the top of the rock face.

IV

THE RELIEFS AT PARSA

The Reliefs and Their Makers

The builders of the structures combined influences, styles, and details from several regions into a cohesive, distinctive architecture. In much the same way the designers and carvers of the reliefs drew on a composite background to create scenes with internal consistency and distinction. The scenes are primarily depictions of rituals and, as such, are charged with formality and ceremonialism. There is no suggestion of the time and space in which the rituals took place: extraneous details which might have given clues are absent. The scenes well express an aura of pomp and circumstance. The technical execution is always adequate, while in areas of particular moment it is of the highest quality. Finally, in spite of the pervading formality of the scenes, details appear which reflect the affectionate interest of the carvers in their subjects.

The slightly rough surfaces left by the use of toothed chisels were more suitable for the retention of applied colors than were highly polished surfaces. This point is made to support the belief that color filled in areas between figures. However, Ernst Herzfeld, the first scientific excavator of Parsa, believed that color spread over all the reliefs. An Ahuramazda symbol in the Throne Hall, as it was newly uncovered by Herzfeld, revealed that its surface had been coated with turquoise blue, light scarlet red, golden or orange yellow, deep purple, lapis lazuli blue, and a few touches of emerald green, all on a black background. In addition, reliefs that he uncovered in the Triple Portal displayed purple red and turquoise blue, together with the application of a metal, possibly gold. Herzfeld was using purely descriptive words for colors, since neither turquoise nor lapis lazuli will, when ground, produce a coloring matter. Other minerals will, however, and vegetable dyes may well

Ruins of the Palace of Xerxes, looking southwest. Larger than the Palace of Darius, it is essentially an expanded version of the same plan. (Persian Gulf Command)

have been employed. Elsewhere, red paint still clings to the lips of guards. Ornaments were also attached to the figures in relief, although this fashion may not have been employed until the time of Xerxes. On figures of the ruler in the Triple Portal there are slits in the sides of the carved crowns into which gold bands or fillets were inserted, and the royal figures of the tachara display holes for fastening gold bracelets and necklaces. Other items, such as earrings, were almost certainly attached to the figures of the rulers and to the symbols of Ahuramazda, while the rulers may have had beards of bronze and lapis lazuli. Evidence for the earlier practice of inlaying statuary with gold and lapis lazuli is said to come from Urartu.

Figures in relief in the so-called harem display lightly incised designs, which spread over areas of their costumes. These designs include a procession of lions and a pattern of rosettes, clearly intended to guide the painters who colored the reliefs.

The visitor who finds great satisfaction in the monotone surfaces of the reliefs of the apadana stairways would certainly be surprised to learn that nearly all these surfaces were originally coated in bright colors. Let us say that he is a country cousin of the visitor to the Parthenon who would be equally astonished if he knew that all the relief sculptures of that monument were painted in bright colors. As an aside, it should be said that colors fade with the intensity of light, that is, colors appear brighter under a cloudy, dull sky than they do under the bright suns that shine on Greece and Iran.

Where did the artisans, craftsmen, and laborers who erected and decorated the structures of Parsa come from?

Fairly early in his reign Darius ordered the construction of a hadish at Susa; the details of its construction and decoration were recorded in Old Persian on a tablet of fired clay, which was found during the excavation of the structure. The inscription has been dated between 494 and 490 on the grounds that the father of Darius, Hystaspes, who is mentioned in the inscription, died in 490 and that the Carians and Ionians who brought the timber from Babylonia were probably deported after the fall of Miletus (Asia Minor) in 494. A translation by Roland G. Kent[1] of that part which mentions the workmen follows:

> ... the sun-dried brick was molded—the Babylonian people—it did. The cedar timber, this—a mountain by name Lebanon—from there it was brought. The Assyrian people, it brought it to Babylon, from Babylon,

[1] *Old Persian: Grammar, Texts, Lexicon.*

The Palace of Xerxes, looking north. Located on the highest level of the platform, the palace has been badly ravaged by looters and the elements. (Persian Gulf Command)

the Carians and Ionians brought it to Susa. The *yaka* timber was brought from Gandara and from Carmania. The gold was brought from Sardis and from Bactria, which here was wrought, the precious stone lapis lazuli and carnelian which was wrought here, this was brought from Sogdiana. The precious stone turquoise this was brought from Chorasmia which was wrought here. The silver and the ebony were brought from Egypt. The ornamentation with which the wall was adorned, from Ionia that was brought. The ivory which was wrought here, was brought from Ethiopia, from Sind, and from Arachosia. The stone columns which were here wrought, a village by name Abiradu in Elam—from there were brought. The stonecutters who wrought the stone, those were Ionians and Sardians. The goldsmiths who wrought the gold, those were Medes and Egyptians. The men who wrought the wood inlays were Sardians and Egyptians. The men who wrought the baked brick, those were Babylonians. The men who adorned the wall, those were Medes and Egyptians.

This was an official inscription and, like such inscriptions anywhere, the writer may have taken liberties with facts in order to enhance the grandeur of the king and of the realm. Although according to its words, materials and workmen were drawn from twelve of the satrapies, it may be questioned that this many lands were really involved. Yaka timber, sometimes identified as teak, and sometimes as sissoo wood which was native to Iran, is said to have been brought from Gandara and Carmania. Carmania, the modern province of Kerman in southeastern Iran, has been described as bleak and desiccated throughout recorded history. Arachosia, usually identified with the lower Helmand river basin of Afghanistan, is not at all a suitable habitat for elephants and their ivory. Sogdiana is given as the source of lapis lazuli, although from prehistoric times the mines of this rare mineral were in northeastern Afghanistan, the area of the satrapy of Bactria. The inscription ascribes turquoise to Chorasmia, just south of the Aral Sea, while the renowned mines of Nishapur lay much farther to the south in present northeastern Iran (ancient Parthava).

This royal inscription does have a relationship with the clay tablets excavated at Parsa that record the payments made to groups of artisans and workmen. The Treasury tablets provide information about workmen from the satrapies: an Egyptian woodworker; some 55 stoneworkers, who had come from Egypt to execute inscriptions; Hattian (Syrian) "up-carriers"; Hattian workmen; 201 Egyptians and Ionians; and Carian goldworkers. Only one indi-

Window on the south side of the Palace of Xerxes. The inner surface of the frame shows two palace attendants—one carrying food and the other leading an ibex. (Oriental Institute, University of Chicago)

vidual, a foreman of the ornament makers, is recorded as being from Susa, and this man did not come to Parsa until the reign of Artaxerxes I.

Only twenty-four tablets mention workmen, and in the absence of the many thousands of tablets that must have comprised the official records of the site, caution should be shown in drawing conclusions from so small a sample. It is for this reason that the claim that Ionian stonecutters and sculptors were present in number at Parsa must be questioned: Ionians are mentioned in two Treasury tablets, two unpublished fortification tablets, and in the inscription from Susa. Additional evidence came from two lightly incised sketches on a fragment, earlier owned by Ernst Herzfeld, which was part of the foot of one of the figures in relief. These sketches depicted precisely drawn bearded heads, said to be very similar to heads on Greek vases, according to Gisela Richter.

The Susa tablet emphasizes the sources of the material of construction and decoration rather than the homelands of the artisans. It does refer to Ionian and Sardian stonecutters, Median and Egyptian decorators of walls, Median and Egyptian goldsmiths, and Babylonian brickworkers. Perhaps Darius had a similar tablet prepared to record his work at the apadana or at his palace. If so, it may someday come to light at Parsa.

The Treasury tablets mention 55 Egyptian stoneworkers, who came to execute inscriptions. It seems more reasonable to assume that they carved such architectural details as the cavetto moldings crowning the portals that are exact copies of Egyptian forms. Carians, rather than Medes and Egyptians as at Susa, were the goldworkers. The Hattian "up-carriers" may well have been slaves from Syria who delivered stones and bricks to the masons and bricklayers.

Of the twenty-four tablets that mention workmen a surprisingly large proportion refer to woodworkers, who were, presumably, local craftsmen. The wording of some of the tablets rather suggests that the same sculptors executed relief carving and sculpture in the round in both stone and wood. Mention also is made of the makers of doors of wood and iron. The workmen described as "fashioners of inlays" and "ornament makers" probably decorated the inner wall surfaces of the structures, overlaid the wood doors with plaques of iron, bronze, or gold, and attached details executed in gold and semiprecious stones to the royal figures in the bas-reliefs.

The Treasury tablets that recorded payments to workmen at Parsa indicate that at one time 239 builders were employed, at another 900, and at still another period as many as 1,100 people. In these records commodities are related to cash with a sheep valued at three shekels and a jar of wine at one

The Treasury. Relief from rear wall of the southern portico shows life-sized figure of Darius enthroned, with crown prince Xerxes behind the ruler. The relief, about 20 feet long, is now in the Archaeological Museum at Tehran. (Oriental Institute, University of Chicago)

Bronze pedestal, showing three striding lions, was found in the Treasury and is now in the Archaeological Museum at Tehran. (Archaeological Service of Iran)

shekel; other commodities included beer and grain. The value of the shekel—a monetary unit rather than an actual coin—was about forty-six cents. The highest monthly payment listed in the tablets is eight shekels, but many more payments were in the range of one and a half to two shekels. Some workmen, including women and children, received only one-half, one-third, or one-fourth of a shekel. Such wages could scarcely be called generous, and it has been strongly suggested that they were cash payments supplementing wages paid in commodities and, therefore, were but a fraction of the actual monthly wages.

"Workman," the Elamite word *kur-tash*, may have meant just that, but Richard Frye, a historian-linguist, believes that the kur-tash were foreign slaves. This view is supported by J. P. Guépin, who noticed that the low wages, or supplementary payments, went to sculptors from Ionia and other skilled workmen: if freemen, they should have been among the highest paid.

Evidence for the institution of slavery in the Achaemenid empire, as well as throughout the ancient world, is abundant. Many slaves were given positions of responsibility, and some rose to high posts. Babylonian tablets of this same general period indicate that freemen had to do a year of labor service, and that hired workmen, who came from Susa, were very well paid at Babylon at a time when skilled men were in short supply. At Parsa such forced labor would have included craftsmen who had been deported from Asia Minor, since there is clear evidence for such deportations of peoples on a considerable scale.

Details of the Apadana Reliefs

At the head of the procession walk the high dignitaries of the realm, preceded by chariots, horses, and attendants. Then come the tributary groups from the twenty-three lands then ruled by Darius. These figures—dignitaries, guards, and tribute groups—occupy three registers. In each register the figures are 3 feet high. On the northern façade the dignitaries and guards are shown on the left side of the façade, moving toward its center, with the tributary groups on the right side. On the east façade the composition is reversed.

The guards, the Immortals, stand with the butts of their spears resting on one toe. Obviously they are not walking but standing, in the military term, at parade rest, as the dignitaries pass between their ranks. Concerning their name, Herodotus may have taken up a mistranslation of an Old Persian word meaning "follower" and applied it to this bodyguard.

In the upper register the scenes show ushers, who carry staffs and wear metal collars, leading three attendants, who hold whips and have lengths of

Detail of the Treasury relief. The royal chamberlain holds the badge of his office, a towel, in his right hand. (Archaeological Service of Iran)

Detail of the Treasury relief. The commander of the royal bodyguard, in Median costume, holds his hand in front of his mouth in an expression of extreme respect. (Archaeological Service of Iran)

Detail of the Treasury relief. The Scythian battle-ax in the weapon bearer's hand is carved with great delicacy and fine detail. (Archaeological Service of Iran)

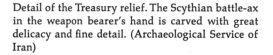

Detail of the Treasury relief. The weapon bearer's sword is sheathed in a scabbard adorned with griffins and prancing ibexes. (Archaeological Service of Iran)

cloth tucked under their left arms. A fourth attendant carries the royal foot-stool on his back. Then comes an usher escorting three grooms with horses, while another usher precedes two empty chariots, one for the ruler and the other presumably for Ahuramazda. The details of the chariots are beautifully executed. The poles are joined directly to the axles, with the wheels attached to the axles by pins in the shape of nude dwarfs. Twelve spokes radiate to the rim, which is studded with spikes. The bodies of the chariots are decorated with incised designs.

It has been assumed that the ruler entered the apadana through the eastern stairway and then moved through it to review the guards and the tributary groups from the top of the north stair. He then reentered the apadana, followed by the dignitaries of highest rank, who alone were admitted to the royal presence. At least one scholar, however, believes that the tributary groups did not mount the platform, but rather that they remained on the plain below and were seen by the ruler from the west portico of the apadana.

The projecting feature of the central staircases shows four guards, with Persians and Medes alternating, in groups flanking and facing central panels. These Persian and Median guards are considerably less than life size, as are the other figures. The Persians are clad in a flowing robe, the *candys*, wear a fluted hat, carry a shield over one shoulder, and hold a lance. The Medes wear a fitted coat that falls to below the knees and is fastened by a narrow girdle, trousers that fit tightly at the ankle with a strap passing around and under the shoes, and a felt hat with a dangling ribbon. The triangular area at each side of these scenes portrays a lion attacking a bull, a scene that was symbolically related to the spring equinox, and hence most appropriate for the festival. However, from what we know of the religious beliefs of the Achaemenids, the depiction of cattle being killed was inappropriate, especially at Parsa, the homeland.

In the long registers of the façades, the Medes and Persians are joined by Susian guards, whose long robes resemble those of the Persians and whose hair is held in place by a simple fillet.

The tributary groups from the twenty-three lands are of much more interest than the long lines of guards, and a number of scholars have concerned themselves with the identification of these peoples. The most valuable of these studies appeared after the uncovering of the eastern stairway: R. D. Barnett and Gerold Walser have been the major contributors.

Eighteen of these groups cover three registers of the façade and five appear on the inclined side of the stairway, each delegation set apart from its neighbor

by a flourishing cypress tree. Delegations may have as few as three members or as many as seven; the leading member of each group is escorted by a Persian or a Mede, who clasps one of his hands. Twenty-one of the delegations offer animals, of which horses, camels, and cattle appear the most frequently, while the members themselves carry precious objects and articles typical of their homelands.

The portrayal of tribute bearers from foreign lands was not an innovation of these Parsa reliefs. Gerold Walser describes and illustrates comparable scenes on objects from Ur, in wall paintings in the tombs of the rulers of the New Kingdom of Egypt, and on Assyrian reliefs. What is unique about the groups on the apadana stairways is the fact that the same groups are shown moving in different directions, on the north and east stairways, thus showing both sides of the figures. This convention was not observed with complete consistency. Figures shown standing behind an animal on one façade should appear in front of the animal on the other façade, but this is not always the case. However, figures with shields slung in front of them on one wall do appear with the shields behind them on the other wall, while the position of hands offering objects is usually true to the convention.

The tributary groups of the east stairway are numerically identified in the accompanying diagram. It should be noted that groups 19 through 23 appear in diminished size on the inclined sides of the end staircase.

The arrangement of the groups seems unrelated to the way in which the lands of the empire were listed elsewhere. In the time of Darius such lists first gave the western lands, followed by the eastern ones, while in the reign of Xerxes the lists showed an alternation between a western and an eastern land. While not always pointed out in the following description, a number of groups wear costumes much like that of the Medes. In the following account the Old Persian names for the lands (identical to the names of their peoples) are followed by the modern forms in parentheses, with the latter often derived from the Greek. Of course these identifications represent the studied opinions of the present writer, and are not always in agreement with other sources.

Group 1 depicts the Mada (Medes), who carry a pitcher, bowls, a Median short sword, heavy oblong rings, and folded overcoats and trousers. The clothing was probably of leather.

Group 2 shows the Huja (Susians) clad in the candys and with the fillet

Tripod bowl made of chert, a hard green quartz, found in Treasury. (Oriental Institute, University of Chicago)

around the hair. One of them restrains a leashed lioness, who turns her head to snarl at two men, each of whom carries one of her cubs. The tribute includes bows ending in ducks' heads and two sheathed daggers.

Group 3 is the Armina (Armenians). One member holds aloft a very large vessel with griffin handles and another checks a spirited horse. In this group, as in others, some differences are shown between the northern and eastern stairways.

Group 4 represents the Haraiva (Aryans), who offer bowls, the skins or furs of animals, and a Bactrian camel.

Group 5 shows the Babirush, or Babiruviya (Babylonians), who bear cups and a woven, fringed piece of cloth and present a humped bull. They are distinguished by their conical, tasseled caps.

Group 6 shows the Sparda (Lydians), who offer vases, cups and bracelets, and a chariot drawn by two dimunitive horses. The axle pin of the chariot is the figure of the Egyptian god Bes. Their cloaks with a corner tassel resemble those depicted in Ionian sculpture.

Group 7 is the Harauvatish, or Harakhuvatiya (Arachosians), whose gifts are very similar to those borne by Group 4.

Group 8 depicts the Suguda (Sogdians), who number seven, have very distinctive footwear, and offer cups, a length of cloth, an animal skin, and a pair of rams.

Group 9 shows the Katpatuka (Cappadocians), accompanied by a horse and carrying folded cloaks and trousers. Their own cloaks are fastened at the shoulders with Phrygian fibulae.

Group 10 represents the Mudraya (Egyptians), who are barefooted, lead a bull held by ropes, and offer textiles.

Group 11 is of the Saka tigrakhauda (Pointed-hat Scythians). All are armed and wear the appropriate headgear. They are accompanied by a horse, and offer a bracelet and folded coats and trousers, apparently copies of their own costumes.

Group 12 represents the Yauna (Ionians), who wear garments similar to those of the Lydians, but are bareheaded. They carry what may be beehives and skeins of colored wool.

Group 13 represents the Parthava (Parthians), who bear cups and present a Bactrian camel.

Group 14 is of the Gandara, or Gadara (Gandarians), shown offering lances and a humped bull.

Group 15 shows the Bakhtrish (Bactrians), who are dressed in Median-like coats and gathered trousers, offering vessels and leading another Bactrian camel.

Group 16 depicts. the Asagarta (Sagartians), who carry folded garments and lead a horse.

Group 17 is of the Uvarazmish (Chorasmians), who hold aloft a short sword, bracelets, and axes, and are accompanied by a horse. The figures in this group are distinctively rendered; the eyes appear to have drilled pupils.

Group 18 shows the Hindush (Indians). All but the leader are bare-chested and barefooted and wear the familiar *dhoti*. They bring baskets containing vases, carry axes, and drive along a donkey.

Group 19 presents the Skudra (Skudrians), including lancers and a shield bearer, who wear Thracian helmets of the type depicted in classical art. A horse completes the scene.

Group 20 comprises the Arabaya (Arabians), who are shown in distinctive

Mortar and pestle of chert, found in Treasury. This was almost certainly used in the preparation of haoma, a beverage obtained by pounding the twigs of a plant. (Oriental Institute, University of Chicago)

garments, offering textiles, and are accompanied by a dromedary.

Group 21 depicts the Zranka (Drangianians), who include a lancer and a shield bearer, with two men escorting a long-horned bull. However, it has been suggested that they are the Arachosians, cattle breeders and mountain people from Kerman.

Group 22 is of the Putaya, or Putiya (Libyans), who escort a kudu and a horse-drawn chariot.

Group 23 shows the Kushiya (Ethiopians), with one member carrying a vase and another bearing an elephant tusk over one shoulder and leading an okapi.

It has been assumed, perhaps without too much verification, that these tributary groups or delegations made their way once each year from their homelands to the New Year's festival, arriving just in time for the occasion. There is no real evidence for this assumption; there may be another explanation for their presence. Contingents from all these lands and from—according to Herodotus—a number of others served in the Achaemenid armies. Precious articles from these same lands were certainly preserved and probably displayed at Parsa and other major sites, while the animals may well have been collected in a menagerie located in a grove of trees at Parsa. There is reason to believe that the walled royal hunting preserves of the Sassanian kings had their origin in Achaemenid times. Xenophon in the *Cyropaedia* ("Education of Cyrus") has Cyrus speak of hunting in the park as confined to a little bit of a place compared with the more attractive open plains.

Possibly just prior to New Year's day soldiers from the twenty-three lands were issued the articles that they were to carry, provided with the proper animals, and told to change into their native costumes. Either before or just after one of the festivals the groups were told to make themselves available to the sculptors working on the apadana. Of course, there is no way of knowing whether the groups were posed directly before the register on which their images were carved or whether the sculptors made drawings or models in clay.

Artistic Style and Technique

Much less attention has been devoted to analyzing the style and technique of the bas-reliefs than to trying to identify the delegations. Before taking up this subject, it seems well to summarize studies that have examined the sources of Achaemenid art, as reflected in these reliefs, with special attention to the question of the nature and extent of Greek influence.

The view held by specialists on classical Greek art is that features common to Greek sculpture are found in the reliefs of the apadana staircases and that these traits are not the result of Greek influence on Persian artisans, but appear solely because Greek sculptors worked at Parsa. Thus, Gisela Richter, an authority on ancient Greek sculpture, wrote: "[the] Greeks there worked directly for the 'Kings of Kings.' They were in a subordinate position and had to accommodate themselves to rigorous rules, which demanded stereotyped forms and 'did not permit the slightest deviation.' Subject, location, composition, types, costumes, were all prescribed." Miss Richter misquoted Ernst Herzfeld, who wrote, "This art is standardized; rigorous rules forbid the slightest deviation." In fact, the views of Ernst Herzfeld were in direct opposition to those of Gisela Richter: he wrote, "In Iran drapery is nothing but an expedient to distinguish the Persian from the Median and other dresses."

As is known, supposed evidence concerning the presence of Ionian and Sardian stonecutters at Parsa is inconclusive. Specialists, such as Gisela Richter, assert that it was these sculptors who carved the garments of the figures. They point out that the robes worn by the Persians reflect the method employed by Greek sculptors about 525 in which the cloth of the garment is shown in stacked folds with zigzag edges. This alleged stylistic connection with Greek work is supported by a technical one noted earlier, the use of the toothed chisel, which came into vogue in Greece about 525.

93

Excavated structure, the so-called harem of Xerxes. Although Greek sources refer to the rulers' concubines, no Persian document mentions them. (Oriental Institute, University of Chicago)

Reconstruction of the so-called harem of Xerxes. Much of the building is comprised of small chambers, which may have been used as storerooms rather than as living quarters. (Oriental Institute, University of Chicago)

There are, however, others who deny that the bas-reliefs were executed by Greeks. Their argument is based on four points. First, if foreign sculptors were so controlled and the execution so rigidly prescribed as the classicists claim, no unfamiliar, foreign aspects would have been allowed to appear. Second, the rendering of the anatomy would have been more accurate had the carvers been Greeks—specific illustrations to support this part of the argument appear in a later paragraph. Third, the Greeks would have been more concerned about obeying the law of isocephaly, that is, the necessity of placing the heads of all figures along the same horizontal line. Fourth, the garments with the folded edges are not Greek at all, but represent a typical Persian costume rendered by carvers who were very familiar with the garment. This last point has been studied in an article about the Achaemenid robe by Anne Roes.

It has been generally assumed that the Persian robe was a rectangular piece of cloth with a slit in the middle. The wearer put it on over his head and tied it around the waist with a sash or belt. However, Anne Roes made such a garment and found out that it did not fall into folds that had any similarity whatsoever with those shown in the reliefs. Drawing on the services of a dress designer, a costume was made that duplicated the appearance of those worn by the Persians in the apadana reliefs. This garment was a two-piece outfit: a skirt, which was made of narrow strips stitched together, with the strips slightly overlapping, and with a folded fall of material in the middle, both front and back; and a cape, which was tucked into the skirt and had separate pieces of material sewn in behind the elbows to form overlapping folds of material.

This garment is said to have been worn on ceremonial occasions, as it was not suitable for serious activity. When the ruler is shown on seal stones wearing this garment in the act of hunting or fighting, the cape appears thrown back over the shoulders and the skirt tucked up into the girdle.

There has been no challenge to this presentation of the "true" Persian costume, while another scholar, Bernard Goldman, has not only subscribed to its existence, but has sought to locate its prototype forms. This search brought to light comparable costumes from the so-called Luristan bronzes, the latest of which were cast just prior to the rise of the Medes and the Persians. Other pictorial representations, such as those at Hittite sites, were examined. With this material so well displayed, it seems easy to accept the contention that the Persian garment was a product of the general region. As an aside, it is worth noting that skirts were the proper attire for males throughout most of the

Tomb of Cyrus the Great at Pasargadae. Cyrus, who died ten years before Darius began the construction of Parsa, is credited with establishing the close cooperation between the Persians and the Medes. (Iran Ministry of Information)

Nineteenth-century engraving of the royal tombs at Naqsh-i-Rustam, six miles from Parsa. Carved into the side of a cliff, they are believed to be (from left to right) those of Darius II, Artaxerxes I, Darius, and Xerxes. (*Description de l'Arménie, la Perse, et la Mésopotamie*, by Charles Texier)

classical world. During Alexander's conquests in Asia it was suggested to him that he wear trousers as did some of the people with whom he came into contact. He refused to adopt this effeminate outfit. However, we do know from the evidence of the apadana reliefs that the fitted coat and trousers of the Medes were fashionable in a number of other lands.

There is a striking contrast between the formal, static representation of the tributary groups and the less formal, more personalized treatment of the dignitaries. Examining the tributary groups, it is immediately apparent that there is no sense of communication among the members of a group or with their Persian or Median escort. In addition, few of the groups display ingenuity of composition and arrangement of figures. Groups 13 and 15 are almost identical and several others are very closely related in the arrangement of elements; there is nothing comparable to the imaginative design of Greek temple reliefs.

While the details of the costumes, equipment, headgear, and footgear have been carefully observed and recorded, these records also show a certain monotony about the sameness of the tribute. There are too many animals, vessels, and articles of apparel that look just alike. Only groups 2, 18, 22, and 23 offer distinctive subjects set off by well-designed compositions.

Group 18, the Hindush, provides the most harmonious design on the east wall; its mate on the north wall is a less satisfactory composition, as it contains one more figure, making it somewhat crowded. A number of the groups on the eastern stairway façade contain fewer figures than the matching groups on the northern stair; there can be no doubt that the designers of the eastern stairway reliefs felt the need to improve over the layout of the groups on the northern staircase. This observation supports the belief that the east stairway is later in date. The design of group 2 is also very successful and attractive, with the snarling lioness and her two cubs grasped very tightly to the chests of their bearers; this composition, it would seem, reflects firsthand observation.

There are jarring inconsistencies in the sizes of human and animal figures. Since the male figures—there are no female figures shown in any of the reliefs at Parsa—nearly filled the height of each register, most of the animals had to be shown very much less than life size. The horses should have been taller rather than the same height as the humped bulls, and group 6 contains so many men that the horses had to be greatly scaled down in size in order to be fitted into a very limited space.

Perhaps the stone carvers and the onlookers were aware of no disparity between the sizes of the men and the beasts, but it should be noted that the

A rock-cut tomb, believed to be that of Artaxerxes III, situated on the hillside above the platform of Parsa. (Persian Gulf Command)

The so-called Shrine of Zarathushtra at Naqsh-i-Rustam. The royal tombs are shown on the left. (Iran Ministry of Information)

Ruins of a tenth-century Muslim palace, near Shiraz. Four doorways were moved from Parsa to serve as features of this palace. (Nineteenth-century engraving, *Voyage en Perse de MM. Eugene Flandin, Peintre, et Pascal Coste, Architecte*)

carved reliefs of the Assyrian palaces show a much closer correspondence between the relative sizes of men and animals.

The human figures are represented according to the conventions previously in vogue in the ancient world. The law of isocephaly is only partially observed. The great majority of the individuals are shown in profile. In a few, attempts were made to show the torso in a turning position by bringing the rear shoulder into view. None of the attempts were successful; the shoulder blades seem to be hunched forward in an unanatomical posture. Some figures have their bodies in a frontal position, their heads and feet in profile, another established convention of representation.

The dignitaries share a sense of communication. Several turn their heads to look back at their companions, even touching their shoulders, while others clasp hands. There is an air of informality among those individuals with hands on sword hilts or holding out flowers. This spirit of camaraderie is in effective contrast with the sober and soldierly demeanor of the long files of guards.

The anatomical details of the figures are rather indifferently rendered. Heads are usually set directly on the shoulders; only occasionally does a length of neck appear. Hands lack wrists to join them to arms and are blockily rendered, while feet join legs without the intermediary of ankles. The upper arms are too short, the elbows ending about the waistline; the hands are too small

99

His Imperial Majesty Mohammed Riza Pahlavi and Empress Farah inspecting the Palace of Xerxes. In the 1940's the Iranian government took over the responsibility for excavating Parsa. (Michael Teague)

in relation to the rest of the body, and torsos do not taper from shoulders to waist. This careless treatment of the anatomy of men and beasts has been offered, as previously mentioned, as a point in the argument against the presence of Greek sculptors at Parsa.

The heads of the figures display a considerable variety of beard and hair styles. The beards of the dignitaries are intermediate in length between the very long beards of the rulers and the short beards of the guards. Most of their features seem to have been cast in the same mold, but a happy exception appears in the members of the Ethiopian delegation who have distinctly negroid features and hair.

As earlier stated, the completed figures were finely dressed with toothed chisels. Next they were polished to a high sheen by rubbing abrasive stones over the surface. This polishing served to soften the hard, sharp edges of the incised detail. The polishing did not obliterate the marks of the toothed chisels on the backgrounds between the figures, and the slight roughness may have been retained to better hold coloring material.

The Triple Portal Reliefs

The Triple Portal was approached on the north by yet another of the stair-cases decorated with bas-reliefs. Long buried by debris, the details of these stairs are well preserved and display compositions that differ from those of the apadana stairs. While the central panel, or element, shows the usual arrangement of guards facing a panel with lions and bulls in conflict in the corner angles, the outer faces of the stair have the animals in the more conspicuous positions with the guards at the corners.

Carefully planned to fit precisely across the length of the façade of the Triple Portal, the stairway sacrificed space for carved reliefs in order to fulfill its primary function of enabling people to get from one level to another. The most interesting of its reliefs are those that are less easily seen and photographed, that is, the rows of dignitaries marching up both sides of the stairs.

By ones and by twos, some 152 dignitaries are shown ascending each of these stairs, with half—the Medes—on one side, and the Persians on the other. The designers of these reliefs, in a bold effort to convey a sense of informality, went so far that the effect verges on the comic. This is particularly true of the figures of the Medes, which display many unusual and charming details. Some figures march along self-consciously, some seem to find that it takes a lot of doing to get up one step, others turn to look at those behind them, even holding out a helping hand. Others steady themselves by resting hands on shoulders ahead, and some stroke their beards. Nearly all carry flowers, held tightly or sniffed at with pleasure, except for one man who carefully extends a large fruit.

The informal treatment of these figures is similar to the handling of the figures of the dignitaries on the long façades of the apadana stairways. It is now generally assumed that the Triple Portal was completed while work continued on the apadana. If such is the case, these stairs could be earlier than the east stair of the apadana. The latter stairway has guards rather than lines of dignitaries marching up the steps. As charming as some of the vignettes of the dignitaries on the Triple Portal steps are, the fact may have been that the total effect was considered unsatisfactory and was not repeated. What was unsatisfactory? In order to comply with the law of isocephaly some of the figures took on distorted proportions, because the distance from the steps on which the figures stood and the tops of their heads was not uniform. As a result, the figures became a mixture of giants, average-size people, and dwarfs.

The sculptors were quite aware of the difficulty and tried to soften the distortion. For example, a figure stepping from one tread to the next higher was most frequently a giant, but at places where the figures could be crowded together, this same stepping figure appears as a dwarf.

The technical execution of the details of these figures is less well done than on the apadana stairways. The hands resting on garments are lifeless and flat, the feet are shapeless and clumsy, and the unattractive beards end in a series of incised lines. Some details, such as beards, were never completed.

At the head of these stairs was a porch with just two columns. From it a single portal led into the central hall of the structure; on one of its jambs Darius is shown followed by attendants of smaller stature who hold high the parasol—a symbol of royalty—and the fly whisk. One might think that the ancient people lived within a cloud of flies. Egyptian rulers carried whisks of course, but there should have been more flies there than in Parsa, if one can judge by comparative conditions today. Another portal jamb depicts Darius on his throne, while Xerxes, just as large as his father, stands behind the throne.

The Treasury Reliefs

In the Treasury reliefs Darius is shown seated on a high-backed chair, his feet planted firmly on a footstool. One hand holds a long slender staff, the other grasps a lotus flower with two buds. Xerxes stands behind his father on the same low platform that supports the throne. He wears the same long robe and the tiara, carries a lotus, and, like his father, sports the very long, square-cut beard of royalty. The crown prince makes a gesture of worship to Darius with a hand that is beautifully carved.

Before the throne are two very elaborate incense burners on tall stands; chains attach the covers of the burners to their stands. Just behind them appears an individual, his hand to his mouth in an expression of extreme respect. It has been suggested that he is the *hazarpat*, the commander of the royal bodyguard. Since he is dressed in Median costume it is possible that he can be identified with a Median general, Takhmaspada, of Darius. Two Persian guards appear on the end of the relief.

On the other side of the bas-relief, behind Xerxes, appears the royal chamberlain, a very important official of the court. Possibly he is a eunuch. His chin—bearded or beardless—is concealed by an elaborate headdress, the *baschlyk*, which is the same headdress worn by the servants carrying food on the reliefs of the palaces. In his right hand, the chamberlain holds his badge of office, a piece of cloth that has been erroneously described as a napkin. Actually it is a towel. In ancient times food was eaten with the fingers. Before and after meals a basin was passed around with a towel with which to dry wet hands. Napkins for use during meals were still unknown.

The towel bearer is followed by the personal weapon bearer of the ruler, who carries the battle-ax and bow case; he may have been Aspachana, the weapon bearer named on the tomb of Darius. The objects carried by this official are carved with great delicacy and fine detail. His left hand holds the strap of the bow case, which hangs over his shoulder and ends in a bird's head. His right hand holds a Scythian battle-ax; one side of the metal head is in the shape of a fish coming out of the mouth of a duck and the other is anvil shaped. On his right thigh is a short sword, the scabbard hung by a leather strap from the sagging double belt fastened by a rosette; a huge rivet holds the weapon to a projecting attachment ornamented by lotus blossoms. The handle of the sword is a flattened oval, the grip marked by two horizontal grooves and by square and triangular incisions. The blade is hidden in the scabbard, which is elaborately ornamented. The upper third of the scabbard, bow-shaped, is adorned with two rampant griffins, back to back but with faces turned and glaring at each other; the face is that of a hawk and the body and forepaws are those of a lion; the feet are clawed. The remaining two-thirds illustrate nine male ibexes prancing within a highly decorated border. At the tip of the scabbard is a bull's head, its horn forming a heart-shaped blossom within nine petals; below it is the conventionalized lion. The scabbard is prevented from swinging by a braided leather strap that passes around the right knee. Behind this official appear Persian guards. The scene took place under a baldachin of which only the poles and some of the tassels remain; this canopy was on a higher register whose blocks have not survived.

V

PARSA: FROM ITS BURNING UNTIL TODAY

Islamic and European Accounts

Not too long after the burning of Parsa by Alexander in 330 B.C. elements of the site and its environs were reoccupied by the Persians. One or more palaces were crudely rebuilt for occupancy, such as structure H, and the settlement of Stakhra, a few miles to the north, was rebuilt and occupied under the related name of Istakhr. It became an important city for some centuries prior to its destruction by the invading Arab armies of Islam in the seventh century A.D. Its existence is testified to by two engravings in the Pahlavi language of the Sassanian period at Parsa. One engraving marked the second year of the reign of Shapur II (A.D. 312), and two nobles engraved the other in his honor. These inscriptions, as well as all later ones until almost modern times, were cut or incised on the walls of the palace of Darius. In this same period incised sketches of Sassanian princes on horseback were executed in the so-called harem of Xerxes.

During the many centuries of the Islamic period, that is, from the seventh century until the present day, many distinguished visitors have recorded their trips to Parsa. The earliest of them, the Amir Abu Shuja' 'Adud al-Dawla Fanna Khusraw, the Buwayhid ruler whose first residence was at Shiraz, had two inscriptions carved in 344/955. (In the references, the first numeral is that of the Muslim lunar year, the second that of the Gregorian calendar.) These recorded that two persons were presented to him who read what was inscribed on the monuments. One of them was called Marasfand, the *mudab* of Kazerun, in the inscription. At this period Zoroastrianism was still flourishing in this region, and this mudab, a religious official, was quite capable of reading the Pahlavi inscriptions of Shapur II.

104

What these inscriptions do not record is that 'Adud al-Dawla took away four very large doorways and transported them all the way to Shiraz, where they were re-erected as part of his palace at Qasr-i-Abu Nasr, a site near Shiraz.

Other inscriptions in Arabic and in Persian date from 392/1002, 438/1046, 444/1052, 462/1069, 562/1166, 773/1371, 825/1422, 829/1425, 869/1464, 881/1476, and 1296/1878. These inscriptions, which include poetry reminiscent of the fatalism of Omar Khayyam, have never been thoroughly studied, either as a group or in their relation to Parsa.

Some of the men who carved the inscriptions knew the site as Takht-i-Jamshid, the Throne of Jamshid, a mythical ruler of ancient Iran. This name had been current for many centuries, following the decline of Istakhr. Many Muslim geographers wrote of the site; their accounts are so similar that a number may have copied from their predecessors without actually visiting the place. Characteristic of these accounts is one written in the twelfth century by Ibn al-Balkhi, which runs as follows:

Next he [Jamshid] built a palace at the foot of the hill, the equal of which was not to be found in the whole world; and the description thereof is after this wise. At the foot of the hill Jamshid laid out a platform of solid stone that was black in colour, the platform being four-sided, one side against the hill foot and the other three sides towards the plain, and the height of the platform was on all sides 30 ells. In the fore-face thereof he built two stairways, so easy of ascent that horsemen could ride up without any difficulty. Then upon the platform he erected columns of solid blocks in white stone, so finely worked that even in wood it might be impossible to make the like by the turner's art or by carving; and these columns were very tall. Some were after one pattern, while others were differently carved; and among the rest were two pillars in particular which stood before the threshold. . . . The wonder is however these great stones were set up, for each pillar measures more than 30 ells round and about, being also more than 40 ells in height; and each is built up of only two or three blocks. Further, there is to be seen here the figure of Buraq [the winged steed that bore the Prophet Muhammad to Heaven on his Night Journey], and the figure is after this fashion: the face is as the face of a man with a beard and curly hair, with a crown set on the head, but the body, with the fore and hind legs, are those of a bull, and the tail is a bull's tail. Now all these columns had borne originally upper stories erected on their summits, but of these buildings no trace now remains. . . . Everywhere and

105

about may be seen the sculptured portrait of Jamshid, as a powerful man with a well-grown beard, a handsome face, and curly hair. In many places his likeness has been so set that he faces to the sun. In one hand he holds a staff, and in the other a censer, in which incense is burning, and he is worshiping the sun. In other places he is represented with his left hand grasping the neck of a lion, or else seizing a wild ass by the head, or again he holds a hunting-knife, which he has plunged into the belly of the lion or unicorn aforesaid.

This account certainly reflects a careful tour through the site. Among the mythical rulers of ancient Iran Jamshid was renowned as a mighty hunter, and it has been suggested that it was the sight of the reliefs depicting lions attacking bulls on the north stairway of the apadana that led to attaching his name to the site.

One of the earliest European visitors to the site was Josafa Barbaro, who was there about 1474. Here is his account in a translation made from the Italian about 1550:

> ... and there appeareth a rounde hyll which on thone side seemeth to be cutt and made in a fronte of vj paces high: on the toppe whereof is a plaine, and rounde about xl pillers called Cilminar [Chehelminar], which in their tongue signifieth xl pillers, every one whereof is xx yardes long and as thicke as iij can embrace; but some of them arr decaied. Nevertheles, by that which remayneth it appereth to have been a very faire monument; for, vpon this plaine there is a mightie stone of one peece, on which arr many ymages of men graven as great as gyaunts, and above all the rest one ymage like vnto that that we resemble to God the Father in a cercle, who in either hande holdeth a globe, vnder whom arr other litle ymages, and before hym the ymage of a man leanyng on an arche, which they saie was the figure of SALOMON. Vnder them arr many other ymages, which seeme to susteigne those that be above. Amongest whom there is one that seemeth to have a Popes myter on his hedde, holding vp his hand open as though he ment to blesse all that arr vnder him; lick as they looking towardes hym seeme also to gape for his blisseng.

Although brief, this description is sufficiently precise for us to identify the symbol of Ahuramazda, and a relief of a ruler upheld on his throne. It is of interest to see how he found Christian elements in the reliefs, much as the Muslim visitors saw signs of Islam.

The Excavators

Mo'tamed ad-Dawla Farhad Mirza was the first excavator of Parsa. An uncle of the ruler of the period, Nasir ad-Din Shah, he was named governor of the province of Fars, with his seat at Shiraz, in 1876. Farhad Mirza's administration was oppressive and unpopular, as he was said to have had no less than seven hundred hands cut off for various offenses. About two years later, according to the inscription that was drafted by his son, he began digging at the site. Possibly his curiosity had been aroused by the increasing number of foreign visitors, and his avidity by thoughts of buried treasure. He is known to have employed some six hundred workmen, but seems to have kept no record of his effort. His digging was apparently limited to clearing the main area of the Throne Hall and heaping the debris around its sides.

Very probably Farhad Mirza availed himself of the services of a certain Muhammad Nasir Mirza Forsat Husayn Shirazi, who was proud of his pen name of Forsat, or "Opportunity." His major work, *Athar-i-Ajam*, or "The Relics of Persia," was lithographed in Bombay in 1896. The many pages of the work devoted to Parsa, together with a plan and numerous drawings made by the author, include Persian translations from the German of F. Spiegel, the scholar who made pioneer translations of Old Persian inscriptions.

Visitors in the eighteenth and early nineteenth centuries, prior to the invention and popularity of photography, produced useful descriptions and engravings. Some such visitors were, in fact, expeditions, complete with artists, who sketched the ruins of Parsa and other subjects. These sketches, brought back to Europe, were turned over to engravers and lithographers, who were more than willing to use their imagination in filling in elements missing in the sketches.

As early as the end of the eighteenth century, visitors began to carve their names in conspicuous places, the preferred place being the gateway All Lands, and a number of them made off with fragments of the reliefs, largely from the easily accessible top register of the north stairway of the apadana. Two scholars, R. D. Barnett and L. Vanden Berghe, have traced many of these stones to their present locations in museums and private collections.

James Morier, a British diplomat, traveler, and author—best known for his picaresque novel, *The Adventures of Hajji Baba of Isfahan*—did some digging at the site in 1815. Then, in 1891 W. H. Blundell, another Englishman, dug in several places, with his account indicating that he found nothing of material value.

In 1924 the government of Iran asked the late Ernst Herzfeld, a renowned architect, archaeologist, and linguist, to prepare a detailed report that would include a description of the ruins and suggestions for their preservation, would offer a project for excavations, and would include a plan of the site together with a reconstructed plan. Herzfeld prepared such a report and it was published in French and Persian. He gave an estimate of the length of time required and the cost involved of excavating the site; an estimate that was to be exceeded many times over in later years.

It was the result of the initiative of Professor James Henry Breasted, famed Egyptologist and founder of the Oriental Institute of the University of Chicago, that excavations were undertaken. An expedition, directed by Ernst Herzfeld, began work at the site in 1931. In his first season a large part of the building that he called the harem of Xerxes was excavated and work was started on its rebuilding as living quarters for the excavators and as a museum for objects from the site and its vicinity. This rebuilding was along very similar lines to the method of construction, described earlier, of the apadana. The season of 1932 was marked by the major discovery of the east stairway of the apadana. Also, the gateway All Lands was cleared and part of the Triple Portal uncovered. The third and fourth seasons were largely devoted to clearing the area between the apadana and the Throne Hall. In 1935 the late Erich F. Schmidt, an excavator with previous experience in Iran, took over as head of the expedition and digging continued under his leadership until the fall of 1939 when the outbreak of World War II brought a halt to the work. The very extensive area of the Treasury was excavated and the two remarkable reliefs showing Darius giving audience were found. The Throne Hall and its surroundings were cleared and its gateway located. Three volumes recording the results of all the years of excavating were published by Erich Schmidt, and a fourth and final volume about Naqsh-i-Rustam is in preparation.

For eight years, during the spring and autumn months, swarms of workmen recruited from nearby villages were busy on the platform. Some archaeological sites offer technical problems for the excavator. Many were lived in for centuries and each level of occupation must be carefully uncovered and studied. Others, such as Herculaneum, were occupied only during a single historical period, but the task of uncovering complete structures and their furnishings is a very painstaking one. At Parsa the excavators had no such problems; their main task was to remove the wind-blown dust of centuries and the mounds of stone chips and other refuse from the building operations. Spur lines of a narrow gauge railway, its dump cars easily pushed by hand, joined a main line that carried all the debris some distance from the platform, where it was dumped on sterile soil (earth that had been tested by trial trenches to make certain that there were no ancient remains beneath the surface).

Only as the excavators neared the levels of rooms and halls did the tempo of the work slow down so that objects, however small, that lay on, or in, fallen debris just above these surfaces would be found.

In the 1940's the Archaeological Service of Iran, directed by André Godard, undertook responsibility for the site and continued the work of clearing the platform. Although the work is still in progress, an end to the excavations on the platform is clearly in sight. When such a day arrives the final plan of the platform and its many and varied structures can be completed and one can look forward to the next stage: the reconstruction of the apadana and possibly the gateway All Lands. Lest the purists be horrified at this suggestion, it should be pointed out that the Acropolis at Athens rises in such impressive beauty because some of its buildings were painstakingly put back together again in fairly recent times.

In the meantime, the work of consolidation goes steadily forward. Damaged reliefs, parapets, columns, and capitals are patched with cement that matches the color of the stones. Masons from Italy, armed with chisels driven by compressed air, carve replacements for missing architectural elements. Of great concern is the preservation of the reliefs of the east stairway of the apadana and of the stairways of the Triple Portal. For some years they were sheltered from the sun and wind by roofs carried on supports of wood. It is now agreed that neither the blazing sun nor wind-blown particles are as potentially damaging to the surfaces of the reliefs as is moisture. With the attention now being given to the site and its structures, the remains should not deteriorate. But neither will they arise again in all their original magnificence unless there is a powerful movement at work—a movement powerful enough to bring about the reconstruction of Parsa.

BIBLIOGRAPHY

ARRIAN. *Anabasis Alexandri,* with an English trans. by E. Iliff Robson (London: Heinemann, 1929).

BARBARO, JOSAFA, and CONTARINI, AMBROGIO. *Travels to Tania and Persia* (London, 1873).

BARNETT, R. D. *Assyrian Palace Reliefs and Their Influence on the Sculptures of Babylonia and Persia* (London: Batchworth, n.d.).

_____. "Persepolis," *Iraq,* XIX, 1, 1957.

BERGHE, L. VANDEN. *Archéologie de l'Iran ancien* (Leiden: Brill, 1959).

BLUNDELL, W. H. "Persepolis," *Transactions of the Ninth International Congress of Orientalists,* Vol. II (London, 1893).

BORGER, R., and HINZ, W. "Eine Dareios-Inschrift aus Pasargadae," *Zeitschrift der Deutchen Morgenlandischen Gesellschaft,* 109, 1959.

CAMERON, GEORGE C. "An Inscription of Darius from Pasargadae," *Iran,* V, 1967.

_____. *Persepolis Treasury Tablets* (Chicago: University of Chicago, 1948).

_____. "Persepolis Treasury Tablets Old and New," *Journal of Near Eastern Studies,* XVII, 3, 1958.

CULICAN, WILLIAM. *The Medes and Persians* (London: Thames and Hudson, 1965).

CURZON, GEORGE N. *Persia and the Persian Question,* 2 vols. (London, 1892).

DAVIS, A. W. "An Achaemenian Tomb Inscription at Persepolis," *Journal of the Royal Asiatic Society,* April, 1932.

DIEULAFOY, MARCEL. *L'Art antique de la Perse,* Vol. II and III (Paris, 1884 and 1885).

DUCHESNE-GUILLEMIN, JACQUES. *La Religion de l'Iran ancien* (Paris: Presses Universitaires de France, 1962).

EILERS, W. "Die Ausgrabungen in Persepolis," *Zeitschrift für Assyriologie,* 53, 1959.

ERDMANN, KURT. "Griechische und Achämenidische Plastik," *Forschungen und Fortschritte*, XXVI, 11–12, 1950.

————. "Persepolis: Daten und Deutungen," *Mitteilungen der Deutschen Orientgesellschaft*, 92, 1960.

————. "Die Palastterrasse von Persepolis," *Mitteilungen Institut für Auslandbeziehungen*, 10, 3–4, 1960.

FLANDIN, E., and COSTE, P. *Voyage en Perse de MM. Eugene Flandin, Peintre, et Pascal Coste, Architecte. . . . Perse Ancienne*, 4 vols. (Paris, 1851).

FRANCKLYN, W. *Observations made on a tour from Bengal to Persia 1786–7. With a short account of the remains of the ancient palace of Persepolis; and other interesting events* (London, 1790).

FRANKFORT, H. "Achaemenian Sculpture," *American Journal of Archaeology*, L, 1946.

————. *The Art and Architecture of the Ancient Orient* (London: Pelican, 1954).

FRYE, RICHARD. *The Heritage of Persia* (Cleveland: World Publishing Co., 1963).

GHIRSHMAN, R. *Iran from the Earliest Times to the Islamic Conquest* (Suffolk: Penguin, 1954).

————. "Notes iraniennes VI: A propos de Persépolis," *Artibus Asiae*, XX, 1957.

————. *Persia from the Origins to Alexander the Great* (London: Thames and Hudson, 1964).

GODARD, ANDRÉ. "Les travaux de Persépolis," in George C. Miles, Ed., *Archaeologica Orientalia in Memoriam Ernst Herzfeld* (Locust Valley, N. Y.: J. J. Augustin, 1951).

————. "The Newly Found Palace of Prince Xerxes at Persepolis and the Sculptures which the Architects rejected," *Illustrated London News*, Jan. 2, 1954.

————. "Persépolis, le Tatchara," *Syria*, XXVIII, 1951.

————. *The Art of Iran*, (New York: Praeger, 1965).

GOLDMAN, BERNARD. "Origin of the Persian Robe," *Iranica Antiqua*, IV, 2, 1964.

GOOSENS, G. "Artistes et artisans étrangers en Perse sous les Achéménides," *La Nouvelle Clio*, I, 1–2, 1949.

GUÉPIN, J. P. "Greek Artists under Achaemenid Rule," *Persica*, I, 1963–64.

HALLOCK, R. T. "A New Look at the Persepolis Treasury Tablets," *Journal of Near Eastern Studies*, XIX, 2, 1960.

HERODOTUS. *The History of Herodotus*, trans. George Rawlinson. (New York: Tudor, 1956).

HERZFELD, ERNST E. *Rapport sur l'état actuel des ruines de Persépolis et proposi-tions pour leur conservation* (Berlin: Reimer, 1928).

————. *A new inscription of Xerxes from Persepolis* (Chicago: University of Chicago, 1932).

————. *Iran in the Ancient East* (London and New York: Oxford University Press, 1941).

JUNGE, JULIUS P. "Satrapie und natio: Reichsverwaltung und Reichspolitik im Staate Dareois I," *Klio*, n.f. XVI, 1941.

KENT, ROLAND G. "The Recently Published Old Persian Inscription," *Journal of the American Oriental Society*, LI, 1931.

————. "A New Inscription of Xerxes," *Language*, IX, 1933.

————. "The Daiva Inscription of Xerxes," *Journal of the American Oriental Society*, LXIII, 1937.

————. "Another Inscription of Xerxes," *Journal of the American Oriental Society*, LXIII, 1937.

————. *Old Persian: Grammar, Texts, Lexicon*, 2d ed. (New Haven, Conn.: American Oriental Society, 1953).

KING, L. W., and THOMPSON, R. C. *The Sculptures and Inscriptions of Darius the Great on the Rock of Behistun in Persia* (London: British Museum, 1907).

L'ORANGE, H. P. *Studies on the Iconography of Cosmic Kingship in the Ancient World* (Oslo, 1953).

MOORTGAT, A. "Hellas und die kunst der Achämeniden," *Mittellungen der Alt-orientalischen Gesellschaft*, II, 1, 1926.

MUSTAFAVI, MUHAMMAD TAQI. *Sharh-i ijmali-yi asar-i Takht-i-Jamshid* [Brief description of the ruins of Takht-i-Jamshid], Tehran: 1951.

NYLANDER, CARL. "Old Persian and Greek Stone Cutting and the Chronology of Achaemenid Monuments. Achaemenid Problems I.," *American Journal of Archaeology*, LXXIX, 1965.

OLMSTEAD, ALBERT T. *History of the Persian Empire* (Chicago: University of Chicago, 1948).

OLMSTEAD, CLETE M. "A Greek Lady from Persepolis," *American Journal of Ar-chaeology*, LIV, 1950.

PAPER, HERBERT H. *The Phonology and Morphology of Royal Achaemenid Elam-ite* (Ann Arbor, Mich.: University of Michigan, 1955).

PERROT, GEORGES, and CHIPIEZ, CHARLES. *Histoire de l'Art dans l'Antiquité*, Vol. V (Paris, 1890).

POPE, ARTHUR U. "Persepolis as a Ritual City," *Archaeology*, X, 1957.

PORADA, EDITH. *Ancient Iran. The Pre-Islamic Times* (London: Methuen, 1965).

RICHTER, GISELA M. A. "Greeks in Persia," *American Journal of Archaeology,* L, 1946.

ROES, ANNE. "The Achaemenid Robe," *Bibliotheca Orientalis,* VIII, 1951.

ROESNER, GEORGES. *La première domination perse en Égypte* (Cairo, 1936).

SAMI, ALI. *Persepolis (Takht-i-Jamshid),* 2d ed. (Shiraz, 1955).

SARRE, F., and HERZFELD, E. *Iranische Felsreliefs* (Berlin, 1910).

SCHMIDT, ERICH F. *The Treasury of Persepolis and Other Discoveries in the Homeland of the Achaemenians* (Chicago: University of Chicago, 1939).

————. *Persepolis I. Structures, Reliefs, Inscriptions* (Chicago: University of Chicago, 1953).

————. *Persepolis II. Contents of the Treasury and other Discoveries* (Chicago: University of Chicago, 1957).

SPIEGEL, F. *Die Altpersischen Keilinschriften* (Leipzig, 1867).

STOLZE, F., and ANDREAS, F. C. *Persepolis. Die Achämenidischen und Sasanidischen Denkmäler und Inschriften von Persepolis, Istakhr, Pasargadae, Shapur,* 2 vols. (Berlin: 1882).

STRONACH, DAVID. "Excavations at Pasargadae, First Preliminary Report," *Iran,* I, 1963.

————. "Excavations at Pasargadae, Second Preliminary Report," *Iran,* II, 1964.

————. "Excavations at Pasargadae, Third Preliminary Report," *Iran,* III, 1965.

TEXIER, CHARLES. *Description de l'Arménie, la Perse, et la Mésopotamie,* Vol. II (Paris, 1852).

THOMPSON, GEORGINA. "Iranian Dress in the Achaemenid Period. Problems concerning the *kandys* and other garments," *Iran,* III, 1965.

WALSER, GEROLD. *Audienz beim Persischen Grosskönig* (Zurich, 1965).

————. *Die Völkerschaften auf den Reliefs von Persepolis. Historische Studien über den sogenannten Tributzug an der Apadanatreppe* (Berlin: Mann, 1966).

WEISSBACH, F. H. *Die Keilinscriften der Achämeniden* (Leipzig, 1911).

WILKINSON, CHARLES K. "Assyrian and Persian Art," *Metropolitan Museum of Art Bulletin,* XIII, 1955.

YOUNG, T. CUYLER, JR. "The Iranian Migration into the Zagros," *Iran,* V, 1967.

INDEX

Page numbers in italics indicate illustrations.